PARIS
FOR TOURISTS

The Traveler's Guide to Make The Most Out of Your Trip to Paris - *Where to Go, Eat,* Sleep & Party

By *Dagny Taggart*

Disclaimer

The information provided in this book is designed to provide helpful information on the subjects discussed. The author's books are only meant to provide the reader with the basics travel guidelines of a certain location, without any warranties regarding the accuracy of the information and advice provided. Each traveler should do their own research before departing

Table of Contents

Dedicated to those who love going beyond their own frontiers.

Keep on traveling,

Dagny Taggart

My FREE Gift to You!

As a way of saying thank you for downloading my book, I'd like to send you an exclusive gift that will revolutionize the way you learn new languages. It's an extremely comprehensive PDF with 15 language hacking rules that **will help you learn 300% <u>faster</u>, with <u>less effort</u>, and with <u>higher than ever retention rates</u>**.

This guide is an amazing complement to the book you just got, and could easily be a stand-alone product, but for now I've decided to give it away for free, to thank you for being such an awesome reader, and to make sure I give you all the value that I can to help you succeed faster on your language learning journey.

To get your FREE gift, click on the link or the button below, follow the steps, and I'll send it to your email address right away.

>> http://bit.ly/FrenchGift <<

GET **INSTANT** ACCESS

Learn French Before You Leave - 300% FASTER

>> Get The Full French Online Course With Audio Lessons <<

If you truly want to learn French 300% FASTER, then hear this out.

I've partnered with the most revolutionary language teachers to bring you the very best French online course I've ever seen. It's a mind-blowing program specifically created for language hackers such as ourselves. It will allow you learn French 3x faster, straight from the comfort of your own home, office, or wherever you may be. It's like having an unfair advantage!

The Online Course consists of:

+ 211 Built-In Lessons
+ 99 Interactive Audio Lessons
+ 24/7 Support to Keep You Going

The program is extremely engaging, fun, and easy-going. You won't even notice you are learning a complex foreign language from scratch. And before you realize it, by the time you go through all the lessons you will officially become a truly solid French speaker.

Old classrooms are a thing of the past. It's time for a language revolution.

If you'd like to go the extra mile, follow the link below, and let the revolution begin

>> http://www.bitly.com/French-Course <<

CHECK OUT THE COURSE »

Introduction
Are You Ready for an Amazing Journey?

Welcome to Paris!

Why Paris? This is a city with a timeless familiarity, but which is constantly evolving. This is France's famously insular capital, which draws more visitors than anywhere else in the world. Here in the City of Light you'll gaze out on graceful illuminations, drink dark coffee, and find darker echoes of philosophy. Paris is a patchwork of separate intimate villages – sewn together to create this singular sprawling, breathing metropolis which has a clearer cut character than any other city. Paris is a place of contrasts.

Where do you start? Paris spirals outwards like a snail, its shell split into twenty arrondissements, (city districts) each section with a distinct and different color and character. You can begin with the famous and the familiar, scaling Paris's gracefully symbolic iron-lattice, the Eiffel Tower, before ending up in a street-art adorned bar in a suburban neighborhood, and spying art nouveau relics. Here, you can wander into a flagship haute couture house, hop on the metro and be deep within bohemia at a boutique pop-up shop in a heartbeat. Or bustle through the glorious maze of food stalls in the Marais, following the surging crowds and your nose to fresh fluffy bread, savory cheese and sweet macaroons before retreating to the lungs of Paris, the lush green spaces of Jardin des Plantes or the privacy of a ZZZ box.

You might fall in love with Paris because it's a mad and quintessential mixture of what is sacred to Europe, and yet there are still surprises to uncover after a lifetime's worth of visits. Immerse yourself in the iconic and order a latte at Café de Flore, the hub of intelligentsia intrigue where the likes of Camus and Jean-Paul Sartre spent hours contemplating the futility of existence – whilst perhaps picking idly at a croissant. Yet you'll be surprised by the patchwork of idiosyncrasies and untold secrets which make a visit to France's capital city such an unforgettable experience, leaving you with memories strong enough to seduce you back time and time again.

Maybe you'll be won over by the balance of enduring tradition and progressive modernity: you'll find a gastronomic culture steeped in pride and exclusive ingredients; a familiar tableau of artistic greatness in Da Vinci's Mona Lisa housed at the Louvre; you can swoon at the luminous white dome of the Sacré Coeur, and witness first-hand the elegant classicism of French fashion. Then there's the postcard of the new Paris. Looking east from above the 13th Arrondissement, glass towers punctuate the rabbit warrens of old working-class neighborhoods, where fashion trends are swallowed up as quickly as they catch on, and the city's new generation of creatives stroll towards the Rue Louise-Weiss, Paris's new Arts Centre. If history is held in Paris's palm, modernity and a new enlightenment fizzes at its fingertips.

You'll probably fall in love with Paris because it's alive, thriving: joyous proof that a city can love the trappings of the contemporary world without forgetting – or fossilizing – it's past.

Here in this guide we will celebrate both the told glamour and history of Paris as seen in the films – it really does exist - and the authentic localized corners of Paris so you can share its intimacy, allowing everyone to enjoy a multi-dimensional experience in one of Europe's major metropolises whether it's your first time in Paris or your one-hundred-and-third.

So jump in as all is explained – from planning your trip and looking at where to stay, when to go, and learning some handy tips about Parisian culture, through to what you can expect from each Arrondissement in rich detail; the highlights, the subtleties, and the rhythms of daily life – without steering you rigidly along a specific route, so you can create your own unique perspective of Paris. Think of this guide as an honest, direct and friendly addition to Google maps, with a local narrative in place of the extortionate roaming charges.

Paris at a glance

Paris's division into numbered arrondissements, city districts, means that it's a relatively easy city to find your way around, despite its considerable sprawl of 105km. Winding out from the centre in numerical order like a snail, with the River Seine flowing through its middle, the spiral begins at the first arrondissement, or 1er, on the right bank of the Seine – a haven for sightseeing where you'll find the Louvre and Palais Royal. From here it works its way around clockwise, outwards to the twentieth, or 20ème, otherwise known as Belleville, which was traditionally a working class area but has become increasingly cool and yuppified. Each arrondissement encapsulates a unique character, and has different highlights, must-dos and must-sees, which we'll go through later in more detail in the guide's section 'Sections of Paris'.

What you won't find here is a guided breakdown of each arrondissement individually, apart from listing them by name below – the lay of Paris's land becomes much clearer when you name the city in terms of its quarters and areas, for example The Islands, which are located in both the first and the fourth districts. Geographically, a map of Paris doesn't really look like a snail, but more like a labeled diagram of a human heart:

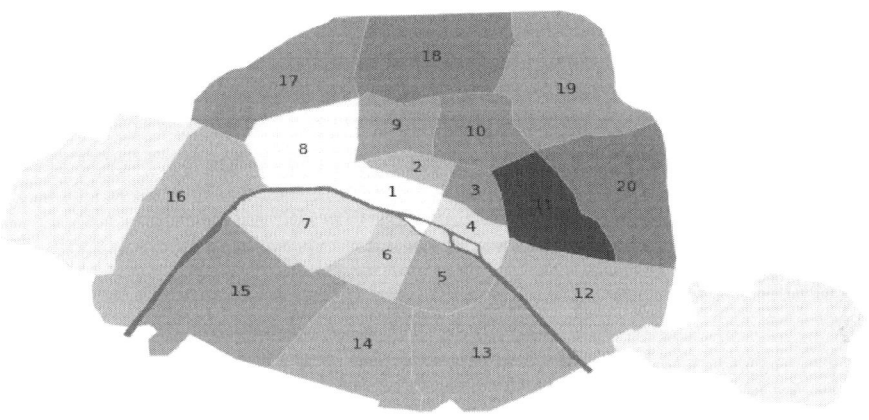

To try and simplify the visuals in this guide, we've converted Paris into a comparatively un-romantic, or un-anatomical grid, which we will feature on each section guide of Paris to help you clearly identify which arrondissements the section refers to, and which they share borders or overlap with:

17th			18th			19th	
			9th	10th		19th	
	16th	8th	2nd	3rd		11th	20th
16th			1st	4th		12th	
16th		7th	6th	5th			
		15th	14th			13th	

How to use this guide

This is a concise and direct overview of Paris, with a very French penchant for honesty – and yet we hope it retains its inherent passion for everything which is precious to France's capital city.

This guide is split into two parts – the first, Planning Paris, will help you to prepare for your trip; giving you a baseline on how to navigate the city, useful culture tips, some accommodation and eating out ideas from locals and travelers, along with a handful of helpful budget tricks.

The second part will delve into sections of Paris, selected for ease of navigation and cultural interest. Overall, we hope this guide helps to capture Paris's poetry without polluting essential information with the unnecessary, showcasing a selection of Paris's greatest, timeless assets along with exploring some lesser-known and underrated corners.

It's time to discover Paris in your own way, side-stepping over-hyped attractions whilst enjoying the essence of what really makes the most visited city in the world.

Chapter 1
Planning Your Trip Ahead (1 to 14-Days Sample Itineraries)

If you could spend several lifetimes in Paris, you would only be relatively confident that you'd experienced most of the city. But then it would have changed again in a few weeks anyway. Just when you think you've seen everything, you'll find new attractions, new cafes, or new markets and museum exhibitions to explore. It's impossible to see the city in three days – as many travelers tend to think they can (we say five minimum to get a real feel for the place) but we have collected a series of sample itineraries together for you to plan how you will make the most of the city of light in a day, a weekend, one week and two weeks.

Paris in a day

Maybe you're trying to make the most of a stopover – maybe you just spontaneously jumped on the Eurostar for a fleeting daytrip. In this overwhelming world renowned city, it's easy to overdose on recognizable monuments, but trust us – this isn't the only way to spend the perfect day in Paris.

10.00 – Straight to the Eiffel Tower

Morning is time to get things done, with a sweet stop on the way: hop on the metro to École Militaire and walk towards the giant magical lattice, stopping on the way for a coffee and a fresh croissant from a patisserie. Gaze up at the Eiffel Tower from the park whilst eating your breakfast and take all the requisite selfies you can. Don't worry, you'll see it again at sunset, and probably throughout the day.

12.00 The Louvre and Jardin des Tuileries

Time to spend some time with one of the world's biggest art collections – but since you're pushed for time, pick a section and focus on it; whether you're fascinated by Monet and Cézanne, or Renoir and Degas, plan your visit at www.louvre.fr to make best use of your hours. Skip the Mona Lisa and wander the Grand Courtyard and through to the bountiful beauty of Jardin des Tuileries, stop for another café (you may need a few) and admire the Arc de Triomphe du Carrousel, cousin to the more famous version down the Champs d'Elysses.

13.30 Lunch in the Latin Quarter

Poke around the intellectual incubator of the Latin Quarter, where everyone communicated in this academic language up until the French Revolution. With the Sorbonne campus at its centre, enjoy wandering past fountains and lime trees and soaking up the atmosphere of a budding generation of potential poets, philosophers and probably waiting staff. Be drawn into second-hand bookshops, and then follow your grumbling stomach to the lively medieval Rue Mouffetard to take the city's pulse and sample delicious budget cuisine and colourful student bars.

15.00 Notre Dame and the islands

Back on the metro to the Cité stop, arriving in the centre of the Seine at Île de la Cité where you can admire the gothic flying buttresses on this gargantuan ship of a cathedral rearing out of the river. For a spot of romance, stroll to the Pont des Arts footbridge to see the lovers' locks.

16.30 Impressionism and St-Germain des Prés

Save yourself for an early evening of impressionism at the Musée d'Orsay when it's less crowded. Swirl through Jardin du Luxembourg and window-shop your way through St-Germain des Prés.

18.30 Climb to the top of Montmartre

Enjoy the panoramic views from Paris from atop the hill of Montmartre, either trekking off your lunch or by catching the metro, and step inside the glorious white basilica of the Sacré-Cœur. Treat yourself to a glass of France's finest vin rouge as you watch the city bathed in the glow of sunset.

20.30 Into the night or au revoir Paris

If you're staying the night, why not head to South Pigalle or Belleville, two of Paris's fascinating suburban hot spots for some drinks and interesting bars?

Paris in a long weekend

If you're inclined to believe the film 'Two Days in Paris' directed by Julie Delpy, then a three day weekend in France's capital can either shatter or rebuild a relationship. We're all for building bridges, so here are a few useful pointers on how to construct your ideal long weekend in Paris.

See above 'A day in Paris' for your Friday itinerary.

In the evening, add a twist by getting your skates on for night time rollerblading. Head to place Raoul Dautry, 15th on a Friday night to become one of the carefree Parisian rollers and join them on these wild rides: visit pari-roller.com

Saturday: Canal ambling, modern art, boating and bistro perfection

Ride the métro to Jacques Bonsergent, and roam along the tree-fringed Canal St-Martin. Immerse yourself in the local atmosphere and wander towards Place de République to make a lazy pit stop at one of many bars which open as soon as the sun pops up. It's Saturday, so enjoy your plate of charcuterie and cheese before exploring the sluices of the canal by boat: either book a Canauxrama-tour, or take control and hire a Marin d'Eau Douce (electric boat) for a romantic day of free exploration.

Friday sees you exploring a bit of the Louvre (you can go back today, and even tomorrow too), so today it's time for a taste of modern art at the Musée d'Art Moderne de la Ville de Paris – a dynamic contemporary art space. From here, you can walk to the Champs-Elysées and marvel at the lights of the avenue stretching into the city from the Arc de Triomphe.

Head up to Les Halles for dinner and drinks at one of the super hip bistros near to rue Montorgeuil. Now, another slice of Paris's nightlife awaits – try an explosive night of techno and get sweating in La Bulle, a hypnotising plastic bubble which shows up at different locations around Paris: https://www.facebook.com/laBulle.collectif?fref=ts

Sunday: romance on the Seine, galleries, and an evening soundtrack

If you're with your significant other, Paris isn't just about lounging around in bed smoking a cigarette accompanied with whimsical pillow-talk. Sunday is for more sightseeing, so kick things off with a coffee in a boutique setting at La Caféothèque on the picturesque right bank of the Seine, and find the quaint romance of le Marais, untouched by the hand of Haussmann, for a stroll. Visit the enchanting Place des Vosges to roam around the Victor Hugo museum.

Whether you're holding hands or taking a solo stroll, Les Passages Couverts around today's Grand Boulevards (2nd arrondissement, behind the Louvre) make for a worthy haute couture step into 18th and 19th century malls in Paris, with rows and rows of shopping galleries perfect for a covered walkway and a portal back in time. As you wander through the arcades, can you find Belle Epoch galleries such as Galerie Colbert, the Galerie Vivienne or the Passage du Grand Cerf?

Be swung into a foot-tapping frenzy on Sunday evening at Le Baiser Salé in the 1st arrondissement, which divides its time between chanson merchants, world music aficionados, and the Paris's most hotly tipped jazz artists.

A week in Paris

Day 1: Walking around Paris

There's no better way to see the city: start at Champs-Élysées for extraordinary views of Paris, through the Jardin des Tuilleries, pausing to appreciate Musée de l'Orangerie located in the west corner of the gardens for impressionist wonders. Catch the gothic cathedral Notre Dame early to avoid the crowds and, possibly more beautiful, Saint-Chapelle church's underground Roman ruins. Head south towards the Latin Quarter for cafes, and hang out at Rue Mouffetard. Visit the Pantheon and head west to Jardin du Luxembourg. Stop, order some wine, sit by the Seine and watch the world go by.

Day 2: Day at the museums

Use today to become better acquainted with Paris's cultural giants: spend all morning at the Louvre, and plan enough to keep you occupied for that time span (note; it's easy to get over-excited, but don't overdose on the medieval art, or get lost). Lose yourself to the Impressionists at Musée d'Orsay nearby after stopping for some lunch, holding treasures by Degas, Monet, Manet and Van Gogh. Happily spend a few hours here. Then make a special diversion to museum Quai Branley, a modern favorite stuffed with non-

European and indigenous art and culture, with fantastic views of the Eiffel Tower from its cafe.

Day 3: Day trip to Versailles

Take a full day out and take the RER to explore the Palace of Versailles and its surrounding flamboyant gardens. The place is huge, and you can easily get lost in the château or the Hall of Mirrors, glittering with the opulence of Marie Antoinette's excessive taste. Do everything in reverse to avoid crowds: start with Marie Antoinette's estate and work backwards to the gardens and the palace. Go easy on the champagne for an early start on day 4.

Day 4: Eiffel Tower

Early is the answer for Paris's most iconic landmark: stop for breakfast at Rue Cler for a pastry and a piping hot coffee before you have a picnic on the grass by the tower and people-watch. After studying its greatest asset carefully and even scaling its dizzying heights for incredible views, take an alternative trip to the city's smelly underground for a history tour of Paris's sewer system. You'll learn a great deal about how Paris functions – and it doesn't really smell that bad.

Day 5: Catacombs & Montmartre

A morbid yet mysterious insight into Paris's history can be found in its underground Catacombs sweeping the underbelly of the city for miles and miles (just how far we're not really sure). Dug in World War II, they are filled with the bones of Monarchists and the echoes of rave parties from the 1990s. Make sure they're open ahead of visiting. Scan the streets of Montmartre where Hemingway and his contemporaries hung out, have lunch here, and head to the seedy district of the Moulin Rouge where you can catch a show or stare at other tourists staring awkwardly into sex shops.

Day 6: Jardin des Plantes and Belleville

Spend the morning climbing up the labyrinth to the belvedere in Jardin des Plantes, and study shrubs ranging from Alpine terrain to tropical greenhouses and medicinal plant displays. Then it's time to head out to the outer multi-cultural neighborhoods of Belleville and Ménilmontant, a cosmopolitan quarter with artists' colonies and strong North African and Asian influences. Explore the nearby Père Lachaise cemetery, where the likes of Jim Morrison, Oscar Wilde and Edith Piaf have an afterlife party. Mesnil-Montant is the thriving centre of alternative Paris, full of little bistros, bordellos and fruit trees. Spend the evening on Rue de Ménilmontant, with its rows of cool bars and nightlife entertainment to choose from.

Day 7: SoPi in style

If you're in Paris for a week, you might want to use your last day to visit Montmartre, having an unflattering portrait painted and coming away clutching fists full of souvenirs. After all the gift shopping, pay serious attention to the foot of Montmartre – pass through Pigalle, where you can return in the evening for cutting edge music clubs like Boule Noire and La Cigale. For a cabaret alternative next to the Moulin Rouge, try La Machine du Moulin Rouge, a hotbed of electro music. Beforehand, root around the often-overlooked quarter of New Athens, home to Musée de la Vie Romantique which houses relics from the romantic era and a gorgeous garden.

Two weeks in Paris

Day 8: Daytrip to Lille

It's only a one hour high speed train away from Paris, so start your second week by discovering this fascinating French/ Flemish city, famous for its beer, mussels, chips and beautiful gabled architecture. For a day of sightseeing, buying a Lille Métropole City Pass is recommended for good value. Make sure you see the Central Lille highlights such as the curious Cathédrale Notre-Dame de la Treille, the bourgeois Maison Natale Charles de Gaulle and Palais des Beaux-Arts, the city's extensive fine art collection.

Day 9: Stay Seine and wander the galleries

Time for a relaxing day by the right bank of the Seine, strolling through the quiet, quaint neighborhood of le Marais (if you haven't already taken this leaf out of our weekend itinerary). Wander through the resplendent Belle Epoch galleries, or Les Passages Couverts, beginning around the Grands Boulevards and winding your way through glass-roofed splendour back in time.

Day 10: Back to modernity with La Cité des Sciences

This ultra modern museum in the 19th arrondissement will pull you back to the present with space, life, matter, scale models of satellites, planes and robots. It can often get very busy here (reigning in five million visitors a year) so try to get in here early, and mid-week to avoid crowds. You can spend all day at the science museum, and grab the chance to experience weightlessness – it's an exciting journey, and it means you can have more food and wine later.

Day 11: Pompidou and Place des Vosges

The Pompidou centre is one of Paris's most daring and popular galleries, with its radical appearance and crazed, stripped down design giving it the look of a building turned inside out. With an excess of 65,000 works of modern European art, there is a lot to keep you occupied. The transparent escalator on the outside of the building also offers superb views of the city. Afterwards spend some time at nearby Place des Vosges, a square fringed with a beautiful fortification of pink-bricked architecture, up-market fashion and antique shops.

Day 12: Disneyland

Whether you're with the kids or you're way past the age considered acceptable for chasing Mickey Mouse around a giant animated theme park, there's no excuse for not indulging in Disneyland Paris if you're here for two weeks. In a day, you can experience the best bits of the two parks, Parc Disneyland and Disney Entertainment Village, with Fantasyland for young kids and the Rock 'n' Rollercoaster for everyone else's thrills. Plummeting from the top of the 13 storey Tower of Terror is an experience of sheer terror or exhilaration, depending on your perspective.

Day 13: Giverny

Take the Paris/ Rouen/ Le Havre line on the RER to Vernon, then catch a shuttle bus to Giverny – Monet's paradisiacal garden bursting with flowers and the home which inspired a whole generation of Impressionist painting. Here you'll find the famous water lilies floating in a pond teeming with life, along with the iconic bridge and the pink fairytale house where the artist lived. Also make sure you see the Musée des Impressionnismes Giverny which showcases the artists who were influenced and followed in the Monet's footsteps whilst passing through the little town.

Day 14: Literary Paris in St-Germain des Prés

Whether you're flying the following day or you're just ready for a rest after two days of day tripping outside central Paris, St-Germain des Prés was once a hotbed of existential meet-ups, literary geniuses and artistic masters, a hangout for the likes of J.P Sartre, Hemingway and Picasso. You must grab a coffee and a bite to eat in Deux Magots, with a moleskine under the crook of your arm for effect, where Simone de Beauvoir along with the existentialists experienced their epiphanies. Walk around the sixty acre Jardin du Luxembourg, where Hemingway supposedly shot and ate pigeons for his dinner. It's your last night, so treat yourself, don your Chanel and sip a suave cocktail at A-lister hangout Plaza Athénée.

Chapter 2
The Best Places to Eat In Paris

There's no doubt that you can eat, and drink your way around Paris, with a very distinctive culinary culture entrenched in years of fastidious preparation, routine and perfection; hearty cuisine, haute cuisine and nouvelle cuisine (phrases de-bunked below). France uses Europe's finest ingredients – in fact this country is the EU's biggest exporter of food owing to the richness of its land – and here in Paris, you have it all at your fingertips, whether you're breezing past a Bretagne Brasserie, getting chocolatey chops in a Parisian patisserie, or drinking Champagne's finest vintage by the Seine, this is where the influences of a country of food lovers comes together. Here are a few hot spots where a Francophile can indulge in their every gastronomic whim.

€ - the budget traveler

€€ - mid-range

€€€ - up-market

Cuisine du Terroir

Cuisine du Terroir offers rustic, large, filling meals, often with creamy sauces, focusing on regional delights and traditions.

Georges Opéra - € - 2ème

A lovely restaurant and piano bar between the Opera and the Place Vendome, with an emphasis on affordable, homey, terroir cuisine with some Portuguese influence. Georges really does work there, and he's a nice guy.

Le Château de l'Ouest - Le Restaurant du Terroir €€ - 14eme

Comfortable, cosy and unpretentious, enjoy regional Basque specialities such as sausages and homemade pickles, with staff who have a vast, intimate knowledge of the food they serve.

Le Garde Robe – wine bar €€€ - Les Halles, 1er

Indulge in 'biodynamic' bottles from local growers, favoring natural methods of treating grapes to bring out their terroir - specific spirit of the earth. Can you taste the difference? It tastes pretty terrific and complex, especially with a fine selection of cheese and parma ham.

Café de Flore - €€€ - 6ème

This luxury hangout for the intelligentsia of the Lost Generation is normally packed with tourists, the bourgeois locals of Paris, and you might even spot a few celebrities whilst sipping on a €4.60 café crème. Play readings and philosophy debates are still a regular occurrence, so head down on Monday evenings, or the first Wednesday of the month.

Haute cuisine

This is the basis of fine dining for most of the world, taking traditional French cuisine to the next level

Septime € - 11ème

The décor in this surprisingly affordable Haute cuisine restaurant in eastern Paris reflects the owner's background as a design student, with mirrors, antique furnishings and industrial installations. The food is serious, direct and delicious.

Akrame €€ - 16ème

At one of Paris's coolest addresses, it's very difficult to get a reservation here, but worth it if you do. With a twist on the typical Parisian Michelin-star dining experience, you'll find surprisingly delicious flavour combinations, and bizarre amuse bouches (offering a glimpse or teaser or what's to come)

Music Hall Restaurant €€€ - 8ème

Down Champs Elysees, Paris's business and shopping heart where haute couture is King, this is the place to fine dine on frogs' legs, Burgundy snails and tobacco duck, all in a futuristic setting with a white piano, it's worth the splurge.

Nouvelle cuisine

This type of food is a 70s creation of lighter, small portions with an emphasis on seasonal produce.

Mûre € - 2ème

Here at this cosy canteen just off the Grands Boulevards, healthy is the word. It's affordable, it's self service and it's interesting – and in a bold, rather than disapprovingly ambiguous way.

L'Orangerie de Paris €€ - 4ème
A restaurant with a décor which has your mind whirring as much as it does your tastebuds, this dream food spot on the Ile Saint Louis is one to bring back regulars.

Spring €€€ - 1er

This newer brand of nouvelle cuisine takes seasonal produce to the next level – with a menu changing nearly every day to reflect the constantly shifting palettes and growth of the French land.

DIY and street food

The best idea for those on a budget, and to taste the delights of the people's Parisian fare, nip to the local boulangerie (baker) and charcuterie (deli) to try out any number of national delicacies for a fraction of the restaurant price. Parisians like a picnic for a good reason.

It took a while for Paris to let fast food happen, but now they won't let go of it. Take to the 13th arrondissement in April for Superbarquette, the annual street food festival hosted at the Wanderlust. Follow your nose to Saint Germain des Prés for some delicious smells wafting from the cosy and hip restaurants and cafes in the area.

Foodies on a budget

Wend your way around the Place de la Madeleine, a frequent pilgrimage for French foodies in search of Parisian fare, but those on a budget may blanch at the hefty price tags: right in the centre, though, hidden under the wing of the Madeleine church, sits a foyer canteen which sells delicious French treats at a ridiculous cut of the price. What's better? Every cent goes to a church charity helping the homeless.

A COLLECTION OF COLOURFUL MERINGUE-BASED MACARRONS. OUI,S'il vous plaît.

Chapter 3
Where to Sleep & When to Go to the City of Light

Paris holds a longstanding reputation for being a strain on the wallet for travelers, frequently in the top spots for the most expensive cities in the world – and to some extent, the rumors are true: high real estate prices in the capital filter down to high retail prices. That said, there is still plenty of good value accommodation to be found for both the budget-conscious traveler, and for those looking for a place worth splashing some cash on: all you need to know is where to look. Here are a few tips on how to get the best value and quality for your Euros, an explanation of some useful local accommodation terminology, and a shortlist of places to stay recommended by fellow travelers.

Staying ahead of the game

Since this is the world's most visited country, booking your Paris accommodation way in advance pays in terms of availability and cost – depending on when you want to go. High season is in summer, from June to August, but it can get busy in September too. To make sure you get the best room in the house, hostel, hotel, or gleaming chateau, try to plan months in advance.

Picking your arrondissement

Everywhere in Paris is accessible by metro or bus, so pick a place next to a metro line or a bus stop, and you should be able to get anywhere in 30-40 minutes. But if you don't like public transport – stick to the 1st, 4th, the northern end of the 5th and 6th arrondissements closest to the Seine. The further you are from the exact centre - which is Ile de la Cité – the less expensive and less tourist-populated your neighborhood will be, with the exception of Montmartre.

Hôtels and the star system

There is a huge range in France when it comes to hotels, and some research is required to identify whether you have chosen an ostentatious Hôtel fit for an aristocrat in central Paris right next to The Louvre, or a dump behind a suburban train station.

Paris also uses a star system completely different to the one you might be familiar with. This is a standardized system created by the government to categorize accommodation on the same basis, but – unlike the UK and the US – this basis is not quality, but rather hotel features and facilities, like a check list: room sizes and numbers, sound proofing, air ventilation, electrical equipment and lifts are all considered in the star rating. Cleanliness and a designer décor are not, so check guest reviews.

Hôtel de Nesle € - St Germain des Prés

Quirky and affordable, you won't get en suite in every room, but you will get a beautiful, colourful mural, and a pretty courtyard garden.

Hi Matic € € - 11th arrondissement

This eco-friendly design hotel is full of primary colored minimalism and is IKEA down to the finest detail. Friendly staff and an enthusiastic, creative approach to recycling make this a great bet for mid-range accommodation.

Hôtel de la Sorbonne € € € - The Sorbonne

Freshly renovated with a modern take on art nouveau, this plush, modern hotel with all the designer trimmings will impress down to the finest detail – including the literary quotes woven into the carpets.

Hotel le Bristol € € € - Champs Élysées

Roll out the carpets, rub shoulders with millionaires, and treat yourself to this dreamy inner city palace next to luxury designer boutiques on the exclusive rue du Faubourg St-Honoré.

Hostels (Auberges)

Gone are the days of hostels being solely for backpackers, the youth of the 1950s, stag parties or any other stereotypes or associations used to pigeonhole this kind of accommodation. Now, many people flock to hostels because they offer private rooms, can be found in some great locations for very affordable prices, and are clean, high quality, and often bohemian and boutique in design too. Hostels are even becoming popular options for couples and families. That said, if you're sharing a dorm make sure you're prepared for some late night jostling and party antics – they're good fun, but often with an undercurrent of mischief and energy. See Hostelling International where you can buy annual membership, giving you a 10% discount when you stay in their hostels anywhere around the world.

https://www.hihostels.com/search/hostels?q=paris

Yves Robert € - 8th arrondissement

A unique model of eco tourism located in an old warehouse of a French railway company, which has been transformed into a solar power station, this is one of the hostels which changes perceptions about hostelling.

Le d'Artagnan € - 20th arrondissement

Nestled in Paris's homey suburbs, here is a prime example of strategic location planning: further away from the city centre means lower costs, however it's nice to escape the hustle and bustle – and central Paris is only a few metro stops away.

The Loft Boutique hostel € € - http://theloft-paris.com/ - Belleville

A clean, sleek hostel in the bohemian, ethnically diverse neighborhood of Belleville.

Chambres d'Hotes

Chambres d'hotes are France's equivalent to bed-and-breakfast accommodation. They vary from skytop apartments, to pub inns. Although most travel websites will direct you to a chambre d'Hotes using the term Bed and Breakfast, knowing the local term certainly helps if you're booking on arrival in Paris.

Chez Sabrina € € - 1er

Just a few minutes' walk from the Louvre, this is a steal at (usually) less than € 100 for a double room. The owner is an artist and interior designer, with a particular inclination towards 18th century Baroque art.

Saint Denis   € € - 2eme

This eclectic B&B is enshrined in the fashion district, close to both the mansions of the Marais and the boutiques of Les Halles. There are no lifts, so prepare to traipse up to the fourth floor apartment with your bags in tow.

Rue D'Assas € € - 6eme

With a small kitchen to self-cater, you'll be annoyed about the Latin Quarter's tendency to lure visitors in with its tempting restaurants and bars. This place is reasonably priced though, so you can justify spending your budget on dining out.

Gîtes

Cabins, villas, rooms in a house, self-catering apartments, bed and breakfasts, this is another mildly confusing, all-encompassing phrase: the difference is that Gîtes are quintessentially French, very affordable, and allow you to immerse yourself in a richer cultural experience than staying in a 13th floor apartment in your own bubble. This is because gîtes, as well as chambres d'hotes, are normally run by French locals privately, providing anyone keen to brush on their French the perfect opportunity to do so – as long as they're not away and lending you their living space: see airbnb. https://www.airbnb.co.uk/

When to go

When you realize that an average of 27 million people visit Paris per year, escaping the crowds takes on a whole new meaning. Of course, the city is bustling all year round – but July to August is when it gets busiest - and not with Parisians, who understandably flee the city in deepest summer. From January to March, Paris wears a cloak of frost and comparative quiet: New Year isn't celebrated with the festive party mood of some other capital cities, but food and wine are lauded with gusto in February – at the Salon International de l'Agriculture, a ten day fair of France's best produce turned into meal material. The winter chill slips away in March, when flowers and leaves start blooming and greening in Paris's parks, and by April – the charm of spring is in full swing. Watch out for closures in May, with its many French bank holidays, and June, July and August are pumping with the world's holidaying population. In September and October the Parisians return and the city falls into a lull, accompanied with a kaleidoscope of autumnal colors. The last two months of the year are great times to visit: dark, chilly days and long cold nights give birth to twinkling lights, Christmas markets and cosy bistros.

Events and festivals

From exuberant and avant-garde, and from musical to social, art and culture, there is a long, long list of memorable occasions, events, holidays and festivals to use as a basis for your trip to Paris. Here are a few particularly interesting ones we've picked out to help you decide on a date. They're not day-specific since some of them vary from year-to-year, so make sure you do your research before you plan your visit.

January

Ice rink at Hôtel de Ville

Gracing Paris's city hall until the beginning of March, this is a picturesque way to glide your way through winter, and possibly a painful one depending on how comfortable you are on skates.

Circus of Tomorrow Fair

Catch the world's most famous circus performers and acrobats (hopefully not literally) before they go onto fame at the Cirque du Soleil. Competing for the top spot and showing off their incredible flexibility, stage presence, and ability to create that heart-in-mouth suspense as they perform a terrifying gravity-defying feat, this is a worthwhile way to spend an evening. Circus of Tomorrow Fair is held in Pelouse de Reuilly, in the 12th arrondissement, over a weekend in January. Website: http://www.cirquededemain.com/

February

Antique Books Fair

A flea market come garage sale near the Panthéon, 5th arrondissement runs for a week in February, where ordinary folk come to buy, trade and sell their used books. This perhaps isn't a reason to book a flight to Paris, but it's certainly a worthy drop-in if you're in the area. Remember haggling is encouraged (try in French) and you might stumble across a rare find!

March

International Agricultural Show

This is week when France's terroir (countryside) comes to Porte de Versailles, and Paris rediscovers its agricultural roots in what has been dubbed 'the biggest farm in the world'. The halls of Paris-Expo are filled with prize cows, pigs, sheep, horses, dogs, cats and rare breeds. If you are a vegetarian or have a certain fondness for animals, this gathering is bitter-sweet considering the fate of many of the livestock involved, but there is a whole trove of fresh cheeses and fine wines to cram into your luggage or snack on which really bring visitors close to the heart of French agriculture.

Banlieues Blues

There's nothing better to wake you up in time for Spring than to receive a hot smack of jazz and top-notch blues. This annual music festival in Paris's northern suburb of St Denis is an event and a neighborhood for the culture-hungry, and is a perfect way to discover lesser known sounds and expand your musical palate.

April

Salon des Réalités Nouvelles

Hundreds of French and international avant-garde artists pour to the parks of Paris, bringing abstract art to the public by revealing their latest striking creations: from paintings and photos, to weird, wonderful sculptures and installations.

Foire du Trône

Europe's biggest contemporary carnival, Pelouse de Reuilly, has existed for around 1000 years and now reigns in around 5 million visitors annually, through April and May. Considering that enough beer is drunk there to fill an Olympic sized swimming pool, amid flashing lights, pumping music, freak shows and greasy food, this carnival still appeals to Parisian families whilst rejecting all of the cultural cliches of the French capital.

May

Nuit des Musées

Or museum night, catch the city on a select Saturday in mid-May when its museums stay open to 1am and offer free entry: if you're looking for that extensive exploration of the Louvre, or many hundreds more museums, grab the chance. http://www.culturecommunication.gouv.fr/nuitdesmusees/

St-Germain-des-Prés Jazz Festival

Paris's traditional jazz quarter the Rive Gauche swings with boogie-woogie, blues and everything in between – and the concerts held in St-Germain square are free.

The French Open

The world's best tennis players battle it out for a fortnight on the city's clay courts. This is one of France's biggest sporting events, so make sure you book a ticket way in advance.

Paris Wine Fair

Sip, sample and quaff the finest vintages and new age grape blends from Bordeaux to Burgundy at this two-day gathering of wine tasting and making professionals, and wine enthusiasts. In the ideal setting of the Palais Brongniart, Paris's former stock exchange building, build up a dream cellar collection to cram in your luggage sometime in mid-May.

June

Paris Gay Pride

Hundreds and thousands of people take to the streets each June in what now feels more like a massive street party than a political demonstration. Full of happiness and color, this a celebration of diversity open to all, and there is a lot of fun to be had whilst pushing the envelope for increased GLBTQ civil rights.

Fête de la Musique

Music, music, everywhere! From opera and jazz, to techno and rock, to fusion and everything-in-between. Accordionists on street corners and choirs in church chapels offer free dulcet tones up to the general public, and the event website publishes an annual list of venues. Be sure to stick around in the city for June 21st. http://www.fetedelamusique.culture.fr/

July

Bastille Day Celebrations – July 14th

Fireworks, lively parades and street festivals celebrate the dawn of the 1789 French Revolution and the stirrings of a Republic. Still today, Paris comes alive with the memories of a dawning democracy.

Paris Plages

The city's beaches, which usually pop up in July and are open through to August, are a collective summer event which transform several spots in Paris into beaches with a distinctive theme. Initially thought up by a frivolous Paris mayor, the Paris Plages are now a permanent fixture in the city, so you can enjoy swimming pools suspended over the Seine and sunning yourself in the sand – a good bet for kids.

Open-air cinema at Parc de la Villette

Traipse to modern Parc de la Villette in northern Paris with a fold-up chair and a picnic blanket for an afternoon or evening of cinematic al fresco enjoyment. Showings are generally free, and at least one film is shown each evening for around a month in July and August.

August

Classique au Vert

A couple of thousand tourists and Parisians congregate in the Parc Floral, Bois de Vincennes, to be serenaded by word class classical musicians. Pack a picnic and savour the sounds filling the air through weekends in August and September. www.classiqueauvert.fr

Rock en Seine

This amped up late August festival just outside Paris provides a collection of big names from the contemporary music scene. Head to Saint Cloud (metro station Boulogne Pont Saint-Cloud) and enjoy a chilled out atmosphere at one of Paris's music calendar heavyweights. Buy a festival pass and camp at the festival campsite. www.rockenseine.com/en

September

Techno Parade

Attracting electro aficionados and dance music lovers from all over France and the world, this parade carries the latest and greatest pick of DJs and artists through the city on two dozen floats for three miles, as half a million party goers follow in its wake. The event spans many of Paris's bars and clubs too, so turn up the volume and quicken the pace in mid-September.

Journées du Patrimoine

Heritage days in late September allow you to take a look around 14,000 of Paris's buildings which are usually closed to the public. Have a nosy peek inside the homes of politicians, private cellars and backstage of theatres, and expect queues. www.journeesdupatrimoine.culture.fr

October

Nuit Blanche

Yet another opportunity to delve into the city's brimming art and culture scene for free, White Night sees a generous cross-section of museums, galleries, city halls and even sports facilities opening their doors for free – all night. All kinds of unclassifiable good things await at hundreds of locations around Paris.

Keep tabs on Nuit Blanche in English:
http://www.timeout.com/paris/en/nuit-blanche

Salon du Chocolat

Prepare your senses for an indulgent treat in late October: Porte de Versailles is a venue for devouring and learning about chocolate in all its delicious forms. Chocolate demonstrations by industry craftspeople creating their fineries are only to be matched by tasting sessions. Strangely enough this is a popular event, so buy a ticket beforehand at:

www.salon-du-chocolat.com

November

Les Nuits Capitales

A worthy celebration of Paris's nightlife scene in late November, here's the time to discover new artists and dance all night at some of the city's coolest venues – most of which will be offering discounted prices to those registered on the website: www.nuitscapitales.com

December

High Heel Race

This crazed totter around Paris by pre-selected teams of women (usually) involves hurtling up and down a giant pink crash mat dressed as fairies and nuns near to Paris's main monuments. Aside from a few broken ankles and people falling flat on their faces, this marketing ploy tends to be seen as a bit of fun and a way to win thousands of euros to spend on Sarenza's shoes.

Christmas Markets

Ice skating, festive trinkets, crafts, gifts and twinkly lights: Paris is a place like no other during the festive season for quintessentially European Christmas spirit. Head to Village de Noel des Champs Elysees: take a world renowned venue, string up some blindingly bedazzling Christmas lights and you've got the recipe for festive perfection.

Paris is one of Europe's most expensive cities, along with being one of the most seductive and tempting: fact. But that doesn't mean you can't find cultural treasures in this city for next to nothing if you know where to look. Here's a price index so you can mark Paris up against other frequently-travelled metropolises, and some quick tips to keep a handle on your budget.

	Average costs Paris €	London €	New York €
Meal at an inexpensive restaurant	12.00	14.24	13.19
Domestic beer	6.00	5.43	5.06
Cappuccino	3.56	3.43	3.64
One way ticket (local transport)	1.70	3.66	2.20
1km taxi (normal tariff)	1.22	3.90	1.09

Free Paris

The best things in life are free, (or very cheap):

- **Make the most of free first Sundays:** get your timing right, and you can visit some of the most popular museums and monuments in Paris for free on the first Sunday of the month, including the likes of the Louvre, the Musee d'Orsay, Musée Rodin and Centre Pompidou. Other museums are free all the time: Musée de la Vie Romantique, Musée d'Art Moderne de la Ville de Paris, and Quai Branly, housing non-European indigenous art and culture.

- **Survey the Eiffel Tower at its best angle:** whilst you're in Quai Branly (an underrated favorite), head up to the rooftop restaurant where you can sip a reasonably priced coffee and simultaneously enjoy one of the best views of Paris's giant iron symbol

- **Book your own free ZZZ box**: put together a picnic, gather your travel buddies (you can invite up to eight people) or just a book, and hide away at the water's edge in these private city spaces whilst enjoying impressive sights of the Louvre and the Tuileries

- **Train yourself in the Parisian art of watching passers-by:** it's a philosophical and cultural rite of passage if you're visiting Paris. Put down your book/ phone/ iPad; the busy streets offer plenty of material for distraction, and it's the best place in the world to indulge in this simple human pleasure

- **Parc de la Villette free open air cinema:** make the most of a summer evening in Paris and catch a free film. The program runs during July and August and usually follows a particular theme. Perch on the grass, or upgrade to a deck chair for €7.

Paris for art lovers

The Louvre is like an art city unto itself, but there's more to Paris's creative scene than the Mona Lisa and Picasso. Don't follow the crowds – head in the opposite direction:

- **Photography kicks:** discover the Russian Tearoom in western Paris showcasing vibrant, gritty photography. Explore Fondation de Henri-Cartier Bresson, a two-floor gallery screening films and archiving the work of the acclaimed French photographer. Trawl through Maison Européenne de la Photographie at the Marais, considered by many the best photography exhibition space in Paris

- **Be won over by the romantics:** Musée de la Vie Romantique is a villa located in the neighborhood of New Athens, built by Dutch artist Ary Scheffer in 1830. Here, you can soak up the relics of the Romantic era and spend time at the café and cute garden in an area which once teemed with writers, artists and composers. The perfect secret garden for a lazy afternoon.

- **Hidden modern art treasures:** relatively little-known, find a rare dose of modern art for free at Musée Zadkine, the former studio of a Russian cubist and renovated in 2012 into a sculpture gallery and garden. La Galerie des Ateliers d'Artistes de Belleville offers an intimate taste of the area's unsung talents in a snug, one-room gallery.

- **Art in the suburbs:** it's not always about the centre - look in your periphery to the interesting outskirts of Paris. Crédac in Val-de-Marne gives life to a dis-used factory, with a lively collection of emerging talents and established artists. La Maréchalerie, steeped in tradition, is now an incredible addition to opulent Versailles, home to a contemporary arts centre, located behind the famous palace.

- **Paris Museum Pass:** if you're hungry for culture and planning on a museum binge whilst you're in Paris, save time and money by buying a Paris Museum Pass, offering direct access into 60 iconic sights and sites throughout the city, including the Louvre, Musée d'Orsay and Pompidou Centre. At €42 for a two day pass, it's only worth it if you're cramming, but there's no better city in the world to get your culture kicks.

Day trips from Paris

Though Paris undoubtedly has enough entertainment and intrigue to keep you going for years, the city is an ideal base for a series of mini breaks just beyond the twentieth arrondissement. Explore the grand suburbs of Vincennes and Boulogne, or escape reality to Disneyland, Parc Astérix or Giverny, where Monet's former country house is located.

High speed rail facilities mean that you can venture even further with just a day to play with, so we've cherry-picked a few places reachable within just an hour from Paris.

A visit to Versailles

Jump on the RER for a visit to the royal city of Versailles, a gleaming testament to French opulence which is just twenty kilometers southwest of Paris, and visitable in a day trip – although this could be tiring. Head here in the morning to make the most of Versailles' best attractions without bumping into the crowds.

Headlines and highlights

- First visit the Château and the Garden de Versailles (free). Roam through symmetrical lawns, grand vistas, statues, fountains and pools

- Jump on the petit train which shuttles through to Marie Antoinette's estate, the young queen's country retreat in the northern reaches of the gardens, where she found relief from the stifling etiquette of the court – imposed her own tastes throughout. You can also rent a bike to get around, or a buggy, but you'll need a driving license.

- Leave the Palace until as late as possible: this is the product of Louis XIV's envious splurge fuelled by his finance minister's magnificent Château at Vaux-le-Vimcomte. The King hired the same design team to create a palace hundreds of times bigger – and they did.

From here, without a guide, you can visit the State apartments used for the King's official business. Wander through a procession of gilded drawing rooms to the dazzling Galerie des Glaces (Hall of Mirrors) where the treaty was signed after World War I. Try to find a surface which isn't adorned with gold leaf.

Giverny

In 1883, Claude Monet rented a fairytale bright pink house with his mistress and eight children in the little bucolic town of Giverny, where he found his new home and created a man-made paradise now recognizable across the world from his painted impressions. It was here that he cultivated his famous garden from which his famous water lilies painting arose, and by 1890, the garden had a pond and bridges along with verdant plant life and delicate flowers.

If you're driving, take the highway A13 towards Rouen for 55 kilometers, take exit 14 and follow signs for Vernon or Giverny, where there is free parking, but after Mantes-la-Jolie on the A13 you will be charged €1.80.

Catching the train? Take the Paris/ Rouen/ Le Havre main line which stops at Vernon - fastest trains take 45 minutes – then take a taxi, shuttle bus or walk 7km (takes around an hour) to Giverny.

Headlines and highlights

- Spend some time at Musée des Impressionnismes Giverny where you can learn not only about Monet's history, but about impressionism as a whole and the group of American artists who came to Giverny to learn from the master himself

- The spectacle of the day will be Fondatation Claude Monet, the product of his extraordinary gardening where you'll find rose bushes, willow trees and Japanese bridges and floating lily pads in the pond, all well-preserved muses waiting for their creator to come home.

Lille

Reachable in an hour, Lille is a dynamic and popular town steeped in history, with gabled houses, tall belfries and beer culture all creating a refreshing blend of French and Flemish. With a large student population here, Lille is filled with adventurous cultural hot spots and lively bars to pad out nights, or evenings if you're just here for the day.

Headlines and highlights

- Stuff your face with moules-frites (mussels and chips) and enjoy a long, cold beer from one of the town's historic breweries

- Lille's Cathédrale Notre-Dame de la Treille is an architectural curiosity which was begun in 1854 and remained unfinished until 1990

- Palais des Beaux-Arts is home to Lille's fine art collection – one of the best in France thanks to gifts from Napoleon and Flemish heritage

- Visit Lille's last remaining distillery, Distillerie de Wambrechies making genièvre, traditionally the local staple drink of textile workers and miners

- Swim through art at La Piscine, Musée de l'Art, nearby town Roubaix's old swimming pool which has been creatively re-imagined as a contemporary art space.

Parc Astérix

Catch a shuttle bus from Rouissy Charles de Gaulle and look for the Parc Astérix desk in the RER station - spend a day at northern Paris's theme park fusing fun and education. Offering thrills for the whole family, this is a perfect antidote the Americanized institution of Disneyland, with the park split into Ancient Greece, the Roman Empire, the Land of the Vikings, Egypt and the Gaulish Village. Scream your head off as you ride the Goudurix, Europe's largest rollercoaster.

Disneyland Paris

Disneyland Paris is like a whole city on its own. Families can easily spend a week here with two parks – the special effects oriented Parc Walt Disney Studios and the Disney entertainment village - hotels, restaurants, candy-colored castles and the world's most famous animated film characters popping up everywhere: the whole adventure can seem fairly daunting. Young kids will be in awe of Fantasyland and exploring the enchanting depths of Alice's Curious Labyrinth, where they can meet the Wicked Queen of Hearts and the smiley Cheshire Cat. Thrill seekers of all ages will love the Twilight Zone Tower of Terror, taking you to the top of a Hollywood Hotel before sending you hurtling down a 13 storey lift shaft. Everyone will enjoy the Pirates of the Caribbean ride in Adventureland, where a ghostly pirate attack will send chills down your spine.

Culture, manners and etiquette

Here are a few Parisian home truths to observe, from meeting and greeting, to home visits if you get that far. Young French people frequently break all these rules, but may be viewed as rude by those older or more traditional.

The polite form of greeting is a handshake. Omitting the handshake may be seen as rude, and kissing cheeks is for close friends and family only.

- First names are for close friends too. For others, honorifics ('monsieur' and 'madame') should be used consistently.

- 'Madame' is used for all adult women except waitresses, who are traditionally 'mademoiselle'.

- Greetings and farewells should not be omitted eg 'Bonjour, monsieur' on arrival 'au revoir, madame' on leaving.

- Trying a little French is an excellent thing, but use the formal 'Vous', not 'Tu', which is delightfully informal to some, vulgar to others.

- Scratching, yawning: using toothpicks, nail clippers, and combs; chewing gum or slouching: all may attract glares in a public place.

- Punctuality is an etiquette issue: late is rude for a rendezvous, but early is rude for a home visit.

- Take care at dinner: cut fruit with a knife, but don't cut bread with a knife, keep your hands on the table. And smile.

- Take care with gifts, especially flowers, unless you happen to know which colours and numbers are unlucky. I mean, 13 red roses is an insult, right?

Chapter 5
Getting Around Paris (Without Getting Lost!)

Getting from A to B in Paris is very easy, interlaced by its Métro system which has come not just to link the city together, but to define it. The Paris Métro, along with the frequent bus services and the RER suburban trains, mean the whole city is well covered for flitting around.

Métro

Known for its veiny density within the city's limits, and its uniform architecture influenced by Art Nouveau – a distinctive style of decorative art chiefly used at the end of the 19th century – Paris's Métro wends its way through the underbelly of the city for 214 kilometers. With 16 lines identified on the maps by number and color, and the direction of travel indicated on the terminus, the system is relatively intuitive, if not saturated at peak times. Night owls should note that the last train is at around 1.30am (2am on Friday and Saturday) and the first at around 5.30am.

A few local terms you may find useful:

billet à l'unité   -   single ticket
carnet   -   literally translates to booklet or bunch – 10   -   ticket passes are very popular

pass journée   -   all-day pass

Walking

There's nothing better way to see Paris than by taking a stroll. Every walk is an adventure, from bountiful scenic beauty, to the echoes of history, to interesting nooks and crannies:

Stroll along Canal Saint Martin: a ideal stretch to soak up some local atmosphere, there is a selection of excellent bars towards Place de République and as soon as the sun emerges, people gather around the canal to enjoy their wine, baguette and camembert. Explore the sluices of the canal further by booking your seat on a Canauxrama-tour, or hire an electric boat of Marin d'Eau Douce to stand at the helm yourself.

Get lost and find new things in Le Marais: take things slowly and go and get lost, wander the streets. You'll learn to appreciate the hills and picturesque sights of Montmartre, the small streets of Le Marais, the artistic and high-end shopping opportunities of Saint Germain des Prés and the cool and bohemian flair of Canal Saint Martin. It's by wandering through those arrondissements, that you'll discover the Marché des Enfants Rouges in Le Marais, the oldest covered market of Paris. Take in the couleur locale and smell the exotic flavors coming from the Creole, Italian, Moroccan, Japanese booths.

Escape the hustle and bustle in the 5th and 6th: grab your lunch in the Rue Mouffetard, and walk via the Pantheon towards the Jardin de Luxembourg. Take one of the many armchairs and savour the authentic Parisian setting: long tree-lined lanes, blooming flowers, kids playing with boats in the pond, and the Eiffel Tower peeking through the trees.

On a rainy day: walk through some 'galleries', and not the art variety. These shopping galleries with glass roofs are mostly located in the 2nd arrondissement (just behind the Louvre). These pedestrian passages bear witness to the wealth at the beginning of the 19th century: mosaic floors, glass domes and pillars. Some of these passages are hidden but find one and you'll probably discover even more Belle Époque galleries and their precious treasures of specials shops, restaurants and history. Can you find the Galerie Colbert, the Galerie Vivienne or the Passage du Grand Cerf? Initially there were hundreds of them, now there are only 20 arcades remaining.

Driving

Driving in Paris is a headache so we suggest you don't bother. You've probably heard about the free-for-all game of car chicken which is the Arc de Triomphe, with its lack of lanes or observation of rules around a collossal roundabout with twelve exit points: try it – hop in a taxi, say "je voudrais aller à l'Arc de Triomphe", measure their quizzical expression, and hold your breath as you plunge into the grand traffic circle. They know what they're doing – but imitate with caution – and remember to check the clauses on your French car insurance carefully beforehand.

Other tips

Take the bus (a normal one) instead of the metro. They take you to the same places but for the same price you get the added bonus of a sightseeing trip.

Take a bike. "Vélib" is a user-friendly, self-service bike system. Booking isn't needed, just go to the terminal, follow the instructions and take your bike. The first 30 minutes are free of charge. Is it safe to cycle through Paris? A lot of people are using them, and Paris is becoming more and more "bike-friendly". Paris is still a busy city though, so be extra cautious.

Hire one of the electric boats of Marin d'Eau Douce for an entire day or for a couple of hours (available from 1st of March and through the summer) and explore the north of Paris.

What to pack

Whatever the length of your trip, remember you'll inevitably want to fit in a gourmet box of chocolates, that outfit from a boutique pop-up shop, and a few other souvenirs – a fist full of keyrings you've magically purchased without realizing, and an unflattering portrait you were coerced into have sketched at Montmartre.

Clothes for rain and shine: Paris is not immune to the odd afternoon shower, even if it's spring or summer, so make sure you layer. Bring a raincoat or one of those universally stylish lightweight cagoules which make everyone look like a human bin bag... they're practical. If you can squeeze in a small travel umbrella, it won't hurt.

European adaptor: the kind of item you always end up buying at the airport for double the price. Universal adaptors are a traveler's best friend, but only if they work.

Good walking shoes: we're not talking mountain stompers, but bring a pair of practical shoes you can really go the distance in. You'll find walking in Paris is one of life's great pleasures, and you might not want to stop.

All-purpose night out outfit: bring something simple, suitable and adaptable for evening wear. When the sun sets, Paris's vastly diversified, fascinating nightlife will swallow you up and you will be addicted, even if you don't intend to stay up to the small hours. From cosmopolitan soirées filled with fashionistas, to crooked underground music venues, a multi-purpose outfit you feel good in is a must.

Chapter 6
Snapshot of Paris' Nightlife

Contrary to popular belief, bars and clubs in Paris aren't all Chanel, Hermès and aloof, etiolated high-cheekboned types. The best thing about Paris nightlife is that it's not ubiquitous. Owing to the vastly different vibe in each arrondissement, there is no fixed mainstream scene, but you can guarantee to find a flavour to suit whatever you feel like doing or listening to.

Like every big city, bars run the gamut from Plaza Athénée where celebrities sip suave cocktails with matching cool price tags – to down-to-earth, elbow-to-elbow neighborhood hangouts with late night opening hours and rock bottom costs.

Music-wise, the electronic scene is of particularly high quality here, with a flourishing culture of live music too: rock, pop, salsa dancing, swinging jazz and stirring chansons (lyric-driven French numbers, made iconic by Édith Piaf). Then there's the opera, the ballet, cabaret and everything in between.

- **Be aware of the tiered pricing**: drinking in Paris means paying for the rent space you take up – so sitting at a table will cost more than standing at the bar, just as drinking at a fancy square will cost more than in a backstreet

- **Arrive early:** at around 10pm many bars and cafes (one and the same) apply a tarif de nuit (night rate)

- **Rough costs:** a glass of wine starts from around €3-4 and a cocktail €10-15. In a chic bar with a high end address, these prices can at least double.

Here are a few highlights which make Paris's fascinating fringe arts scene so interesting after dark.

Highlights

- **Work up a thirst at tiny 20eme Rock 'n' Roll bar, La Féline €:** with its own eponymous record label producing much of the music played and posted on the walls here, La Féline is dangerously sexy, raw, and glamorous. Everyone here is done up to the nines, particularly the bar staff, and the combination of tattooed hipsters and ageing rockers is a fun mise en scène – especially because everyone is pretty pleasant.

- **A mid-week bohemian fix in Café Charbon, Rue Oberkampf €€:** in this ever-bustling area of the 11th arrondissement, this cafe-bar has been a magnet for nocturnal Parisians for more than a century. Dating back to the second empire of Napoleon III, the brasserie-style décor, tarnished mirrors and wrought iron lamps make for perfectly obscure surroundings complemented by DJs dishing out a mish-mash selection of world, pop and electro. At weekends, Café Charbon gets overwhelmingly busy, so stick to the working week.

- **Revel in the precious ambiance of The Delaville Café, Grands Boulevards €€€:** open from springtime onwards, this upmarket cafe has the pomp of its past embellished all over it. It used to be a brothel in Napoleon's 19th century Paris, and then a high end eatery, a Chinese restaurant, and now a resplendent watering hole for the chic – wannabe fashionistas, journalists and designers.

Chapter 7
A Bit of History - Paris Throughout Time

We can't explain the history of Paris properly in a few pages, just as you can't see all the historical sights in a few days. You can, though, see some stunning things, and gain an insight into some of the most astonishing events in European history. Here is a snapshot of what Paris has experienced over the years.

Prehistoric Paris & Lucotocia
The earliest human traces in Paris date back to around 9000BC; though it is possible that these were nomadic hunter-gatherers – in fact Paris's first tourists. The oldest evidence of permanent residence was found in the 12th arrondissement: fragments of three wooden fishermen's canoes used on the Seine around 4500BC.

These, and other early remains, can be seen at the Carnavalet Museum.

By 200 BC, the Parisii tribe – Celts - were settled on the Île de la Cité and building bridges over the Seine. The Parisii may have given Paris its name, but to them the place was called Lucotocia. The settlement was the easiest place to cross the Seine, holding a strategic position on the main trade route between Britain and to the Roman colonies.

Relations with the Roman empire were troubled, and around 53 BC, Julius Caesar came, saw and eventually conquered the Parisii at the Battle of Lutetia – the Roman name for Paris.

From Clovis to the Capetian Kings (6th to 11th centuries AD)

In 486, Clovis I, ruler of the Franks, defeated the Roman army and became the ruler of all Gaul north of the Loire.

The Church of the Abbaye de Saint-Germain-des-Prés is the burial place of these first Kings of France.

In the 9th century, Paris was repeatedly attacked by the Vikings, who sailed great war-fleets up the Seine, laying siege, ravaging crops, and basically doing what Vikings do.

From 987, a new dynasty of kings, the Capetians, came to power – they restored the royal palaces and churches and prosperity returned.

The Middle Ages (12ᵗʰ-15ᵗʰ centuries)

Under the Capetian kings, Paris gradually became the political, cultural, and religious capital of all France. In 1190, King Philippe-Auguste began the massive Château du Louvre, designed to protect against an English attack from Normandy. The foundations can be seen today in the basement of the Louvre Museum.

The Basilica of St Denis (the first Gothic church) and Notre Dame cathedral are both evocative of this period.

By the 13th century, Paris was one of the main centres of learning in Europe – the Sorbonne could boast Roger Bacon and Saint Thomas Aquinas as teachers. Commercially, the city was booming – by 1328, Paris was the largest city in Europe.

The 14ᵗʰ century brought bad news: the Bubonic plague and the Hundred Years' War. In its first outbreak in 1348, the plague killed a quarter of Paris's population, and there were repeated later outbreaks to compound the suffering.

The 15ᵗʰ century brought more misfortune. In 1420, an English army and its Burgundian allies occupied Paris. King Henry VI of England was crowned King of France at Notre Dame Cathedral in 1431. The English did not leave Paris until 1436, when Charles VII of France was finally able to return. Much of the city was left in ruins; half the population had departed.

The Museum of the Middle Ages offers extensive evidence and information from this turbulent period.

The Renaissance (16ᵗʰ Century)

Paris had regained its old prosperity by 1500, and each new king added new buildings, bridges and fountains – often in the Renaissance style imported from Italy. Francis I (1534-1547) was particularly influential, making the Louvre his home, and making Paris a centre of learning and scholarship.

In the early 1600s tension grew in Paris between the followers of the established Catholic church and Protestant Calvinism. The Sorbonne and University of Paris were key bastions of Catholic orthodoxy, who attacked – both intellectually and literally - Protestants and humanists. The French Wars of Religion culminated in a decision to kill the leaders of the Protestant cause. These assassinations turned into a general slaughter; with about three thousand Protestants killed in Paris.

The Wars of Religion continued, with assassinations, massacres and sieges until 1594, when Henry IV first defeated the Catholic armies in battle, and then converted to Catholicism.

Buildings from this period include: the Lescot wing of the Louvre, the houses at 11 and 13 rue François-Miron in Le Marais, and Saint-Eustache church.

17th century

Paris suffered great losses during the wars of religion, but under Henry IV, and his widow Marie de Medicis, the city was repopulated, rebuilt and re-energised.

Louis XIII continued with grand building projects, and his chief minister Cardinal de Richelieu built one of the grandest projects of all: the Palais-Royal.

Louis XIV's reign was less harmonious. His chief minister, Cardinal Mazarin imposed harsh taxes which led to a long uprising. Louis moved his royal residence out of the city to Versailles, and came into Paris as seldom as possible.

Things to see include the Medici Fountain (1633) in the Luxembourg Gardens; the Place des Vosges; the facade of the church of Saint-Paul-Saint-Louis in the Marais, and the church of Les Invalides (1671–1678)

18th century

Under Louis XV, the city expanded westward and continued to grow in population – to 600,000. The centre of the city became more and more crowded.

The city's 400 cafés became meeting places for writers and scholars: Voltaire, Rousseau, Diderot and D'Alembert, and Paris found itself at the centre of the explosion of philosophic and scientific activity known as the Age of Enlightenment.

On the Faubourg Saint-Germain the wealthy built magnificent houses in the neo-classical style, but elsewhere, most of Paris had narrow, dirty and foul-smelling streets: the city had no mayor or single city government.

Things to see include The Paris Panthéon and the Rotonde in Parc Monceau.

The French Revolution (1789-1799)

In the summer of 1789 Paris was the centre of events which changed the history Europe. Then as now, wealthier Parisians lived in the western part of the city, the merchants in the middle, while the workers, poor and unemployed - known as the 'sans culottes' - occupied the southern and eastern areas –

On 11 July, the king's soldiers attacked a peaceful demonstration and a revolutionary uprising was triggered. To paint a fuller picture and fill in the blanks for this fascinating period of radicalism, social and political upheaval, spend some time with the French Revolution collection at the Louvre.

Understandably, there was not a lot of building going on at this time, but the Passage des Panoramas one of the first covered shopping streets in Europe, opened in 1799.

Napoleon I (1800–1815)

First Consul Napoleon Bonaparte moved into the Tuileries Palace in 1800 and re-established calm and order.

Napoleon also started a number of large projects to make Paris into an imperial capital, including the Arc de Triomphe; and developed the infrastructure of the city, which had been neglected for years.

Unfortunately, Napoleon also embarked on a series of wars between 1804 and 1815, with initial success, but leading to complete defeat in 1815.

The Restoration (1815-1830)

Following the downfall of Napoleon, an army of 300,000 soldiers from England, Austria, Russia and Germany occupied Paris, and remained until December 1815. Louis XVIII returned to the city and moved into the old rooms of Napoleon at the Tuileries Palace.

The aristocrats who had emigrated returned to their town houses in the Faubourg Saint-Germain, and the cultural life of the city resumed.

Louis XVIII was succeeded by his son Charles X in 1824, but the government became increasingly unpopular.

At this time the heart the city was a maze of narrow, winding streets and crumbling buildings from earlier centuries; dark, crowded, unhealthy and dangerous. Sewers emptied directly into the Seine and a cholera outbreak in 1830 killed twenty thousand people.

The Second Republic and Napoleon III (1848-1870)

In December 1848, Louis-Napoleon Bonaparte, the nephew of Napoleon I, became the first elected President of France. By 1851 he was bored with being just president, organized a coup d'état, and became Emperor Napoleon III.

In 1853 Napoleon III launched a gigantic public works program, under the direction of George Haussmann, whose purpose was to put unemployed Parisians to work and to bring clean water, light and open space to the centre of the city. Haussmann's efforts gave central Paris the street plan and distinctive look it still retains today.

The Siege of Paris and the Commune (1870-1871)

Napoleon III's rule came to an abrupt end when he declared war on Prussia in 1870, only to be defeated and captured. On 4 September 1870 France became a republic for a third time. Towards the end of that year the Prussian army besieged, and briefly occupied Paris, then withdrew outside the city.

In 1871 soldiers from the Paris National Guard killed two French generals, prompting the French government and army to withdraw to Versailles. A new city council, the Paris Commune, dominated by anarchists and radical socialists, was elected and took power for two months.

In May the French army reconquered the city in bitter fighting, in which 8000 died – mostly Communards; tens of thousands were imprisoned, and tens of thousands more fled abroad. Many important buildings were set on fire.

The Belle Époque (1871–1914)

After the fall of the Commune until 1878, the city was governed by the conservative national government in Versailles. Towards the end of the century, Paris began to modernise its public transport system, beginning the first metro line in 1897. Paris also became the birthplace of modern art and of the cinema, during an artistic period known as the Belle Époque. Most artists worked in Montmartre where rents were low and the atmosphere congenial: Renoir, Utrillo, Dufy, Picasso, Modigliani.

In 1895, the first public projection of a motion picture was made by the Lumière Brothers in a Paris café.

The First World War (1914-1918)

Within a few weeks of the start of the war, the German Army had reached the Marne River, east of Paris. The French government moved to Bordeaux in September, and the great masterpieces of the Louvre were transported to Toulouse.

In 1914, the Germans were eventually pushed back by the French and British armies; the government returned to Paris, and theatres and cafés re-opened.

As the war progressed, the city was bombed by German heavy bombers and rationing was widespread: gas, electricity, coal, bread, butter, flour, potatoes and sugar. There were also deadly outbreaks of typhoid, measles, and influenza.

Paris between the Wars – (1919-1938)

After the war, unemployment surged, prices soared, and rationing continued.

Despite the hardships, Paris resumed its place as the capital of the arts during les années folles, or "the crazy years." The centre of artistic ferment moved from Montmartre to the neighborhood of Montparnasse. Painters, writers and poets, including Ernest Hemingway, Igor Stravinsky, W.B. Yeats, and Ezra Pound came from around the world to join the fun. Paris was the birthplace of new movements: Dadaism and Surrealism. George Gershwin came to Paris in 1928, and Jazz was played everywhere.

The worldwide Great Depression hit home in 1931 bringing hardships and a more sombre mood. Political tensions also grew, with hostility between left-wind and right wing factions increasingly evident.

The Occupation and the Liberation (1940–1945)

Following the German invasion of Poland in September 1939, France declared war on Germany. Thirty thousand Paris children were evacuated, bomb shelters were constructed, but cafés and theatres remained open.

The Germans attacked France on 10 May 1940, and entered Paris unopposed on June 14. Adolf Hitler arrived on June 24, saw the tourist sites, and left.

For the Parisians, the occupation was a series of frustrations, shortages and humiliations. A curfew and blackout applied from nine at night. Food, tobacco, coal and clothing were rationed. A million Parisians left the city for the provinces, where there was more food and fewer Germans.

Parisian Jews were initially forced to wear a yellow star. In 1942 over twelve thousand News, including more than 4000 children, were rounded up by the French police, on orders of the Germans, and sent to concentration camps.

There was resistance by clandestine groups, but reprisals by the Germans were swift and harsh.

The Allies landed at Normandy in 1944, and began to advance towards Paris.

The German commander of Paris ignored an order from Adolf Hitler to destroy the monuments of the city, and surrendered the city on 25 August. General De Gaulle arrived on 26 August, and led a massive parade down the Champs Elysée. A fourth Republic was established.

Post-war Politics (1946-2000)

Reconstruction took time; however by the mid-1970s Paris had been repaired and refurbished on a scale that echoed the age of Haussmann.

After the war, rationing of essential foodstuffs continued for several years, and much of the housing in Paris was old and run-down. Gradually, successive governments improved this situation by large scale rebuilding.

Politics in Paris remained turbulent: strikes, demonstrations, and a fractious relationship between the public and the police. The struggle for the independence of Algeria, and the resistance of French residents of Algeria, led in 1961 to numerous bombings and deadly confrontations in Paris between demonstrators and the police. The deeply divided Fourth Republic collapsed in 1958, and a new government, under President Charles De Gaulle, was elected.

In 1968, Paris experienced student uprisings on the left bank; barricades and red flags appeared, university buildings were occupied, and a general strike closed down much of Paris.

Alongside all this, the cultural life of Paris resumed, this time centered around the cafés of Saint-Germain-des-Pres; Jean-Paul Sartre and Simone de Beauvoir held court, and Paris designers, led by Christian Dior, made Paris once again the capital of high fashion.

In this post-war era, Paris experienced its largest urban development since Haussmann.

Crisis in the banlieues (1970s to now)

From the 1970s, many banlieues (outlying suburbs of Paris) experienced dramatic social change, as factories and industries closed or moved out of the city. The once-thriving residential areas became ghettos for African and Arab immigrants, with limited skills and high unemployment. At the same time, some wealthier suburbs successfully shifted their economic base from traditional manufacturing to high-tech services, giving these neighborhoods some of the highest incomes in Europe.

The resulting widening economic and religious gap led to periodic clashes between young Muslims and the police, culminating in major disturbances in 2005.

In 2015, two Islamic extremists, French citizens raised in Paris, attacked the Paris headquarters of Charlie Hebdo, a controversial satirical magazine that had poked ridicule at Mohammed. They killed thirteen people. Shortly afterwards, a third terrorist killed four hostages at a Jewish grocery store at Porte de Vincennes. On 11 January an estimated 1.5 million people marched in Paris to show solidarity against terrorism and in defence of freedom of speech.

The Louvre Lit Up In Late Evening.

Chapter 8
The Heart of the City: 1st & 2nd Arrondissements

17th		18th		19th	
	8th	9th	10th	11th	20th
16th		2nd	3rd		
		1st	4th	12th	
	7th	6th	5th	13th	
	15th	14th			

The 1st arrondissement largely comprises iconic sites: the Louvre, Palais Royal, Tuileries Gardens, with the added lure of great shopping and great architecture. The Louvre is one of the world's most iconic sites, an astonishing assemblage of art and history.

The 2nd Arrondissement houses the financial district, which offers the visitor more architecture to admire but not much else; Rue Montorgreuil, the famous food street; and the fine Gothic Saint Eustache church.

Headlines and Highlights

- **Musée du Louvre** – you may not have heard of the Louvre - it's a kind of art gallery. Seriously, though, the Louvre is an art gallery and museum so vast and ornate and packed with art and antiquities that it can be quite daunting; even overwhelming: Venus de Milo. Mona Lisa... Michaelangelo, Raphael, Botticelli and Titian. Etc. See below for health warnings and advice.

- **Musée de l'Orangerie** – fabulous Impressionist collection, including Monet's Water Lilies, but also works by Cézanne, Matisse, Picasso, Renoir, Sisley, Soutine and Utrillo.

- **Centre Pompidou** – a wonderful and radical piece of modern architecture, with an outstanding collection of modern art, for lovers of surrealists , cubists, and pop art.

- **Jardin des Tuileries** - a place where history and culture meet on the banks of the Seine. Sculptures (including Louise Bourgeois' The Welcoming Hands ') merge with lawns, pools and fountains, while casual strollers – and lively joggers - amuse themselves on the shaded footpaths.

- **Église St-Eustache** - one of the most majestic and beautiful churches in Paris. Built from 1532 and 1637, St-Eustache offers flamboyant Gothic arches, spectacular Renaissance ornamentation and a gargantuan organ.

The Louvre

The Louvre is art gallery, museum, and architectural site-of-interest rolled into one. The Louvre began life as a royal collection housed in former palaces. After the French Revolution, the palace and its contents were effectively nationalized and the Louvre became a museum in 1793. Since then, both the building and the collection have been extended and enhanced constantly, resulting in, well... in an institution. If you are an art student or an art lover, then a lot of the things that you have read about and heard about are here in real life. Tastes vary, of course, but here is a snapshot of what the Louvre offers :

- Leonardo: six major works including the Mona Lisa

- Wonderfully evocative ancient Egyptian art, especially the Chapel of the Tomb of Akhethetep

- Superb ancient Greek sculpture; the Borghese Gladiator and Venus de Milo are the best known of many.

- Raphael: six major works from another Renaissance great.

- Pompeii silver: the Boscoreale haul of Roman silver-work, in almost perfect order

- Vermeer: see The Lacemaker and The Astronomer

- Persian carpets: including the exquisite 16th century Mantes carpet

- Watteau: joyous paintings from the 18th century French master

The Louvre: Footnotes & Lowlights

The Louvre appears in every guides list of headline sights and must-see highlights, but - considering that it is probably the best-known museum in the world - the Louvre manages to offer saddening surprises to a large number of small-town art lovers. Here are the commonest disappointments and how to avoid them.

- **The queues.** It is not unusual to queue for over an hour for tickets at the Pyramide entrance. If you can afford it, pay a couple of Euros extra and buy your ticket in advance at FNAC department store, or similar outlets. Otherwise, sneak around to the usually-quiet but not-always-open Porte des Lions entrance. Otherwise, spend most of the day relaxing around Paris, then hit the museum two hours before closing time.

- **The cost.** A visit to the Louvre can be expensive for a family, especially if you don't want to stay there long. An evening visit offers best value, after 18:00 on Wednesdays and Fridays prices fall. The museum is also free first Sunday of the month, but that's October to March only, and it gets very busy.

- **The size.** The Louvre isn't big. It's absolutely massive. Remember that small-town art lover I mentioned? They probably like to spend five minutes at each art work, and prefer not to spend more than two hours a day in a museum. At that rate, it would take them over four years, visiting every day, to view all the artwork in the Louvre – that's just the 35,000 works of art; there are also 350,000 'other objects' on display. If you are unprepared for the scale of the place, it is very easy to be overwhelmed. Like a 96-hole golf course, or a 2kg doughnut, it's just too much. It is also very easy to get lost, and very easy to get sore feet trekking through the huge galleries – there are several miles of corridors. The simple trick here is online research. Don't go expecting to see everything. You can't. Figure out what you want to see – online; then figure out your route – online; go to www.louvre.fr then click 'plan your visit'.

- **The crowds.** Unless you're very tall, there isn't an easy way to gain an uninterrupted view of the Mona Lisa. If the museum is really crowded, the best option is to plan another visit, either late in the day or off-season. 'Second trips' are in fact a good idea anyway. Many visitors – having done the 'must see' sights enjoy coming back again, just to wander through some of the quieter, less-famous but equally-wonderful galleries.

- **The modern art**. For some reason, some people stop reading after 'the most impressive collection of art in the world...' and fail to pick up or take in 'up to the mid-Nineteenth century'. Apart from a one-room collection - Monet, Cézanne, Renoir and Degas – you will have to go elsewhere for modern art: the Centre Georges Pompidou, or Musée d'Orsay, or Musée Marmottan.

- **The mysterious missing masterpiece.** For some reason, the Louvre periodically re-rooms its most iconic pieces (Venus de Milo, Mona Lisa). There are also frequent room closures (for maintenance) and important exhibits are regularly being either lent-out or borrowed-in. Again, online research is important; but it's also a good idea to ask at the information desk if there is something you absolutely must see.

- **The catering.** Some visitors fail to realise that the Louvre has more than one café (they have six) and consequently pay snooty-restaurant prices for a coffee and a snack. Café Mollien on the first floor is the best priced option in the museum, but... most tickets allow re-entry, so you can just pop out, nip over to a coffee stall in Jardins des Tuileries, then return refreshed for another dose of Assyrian antiquities.

Other places to go and see

The Louvre

Again? Yes, again. The Louvre really isn't a place to visit just once, in fact some people say that you should visit it several times or not at all. The art collections are obviously the main reason to go, but there are in fact three other excellent museums in the same building, typically included in the one ticket price: The Musée des Arts Décoratifs (Applied Arts Museum), the Musée de la Publicité (Advertising Museum), and the Musée de la Mode et du Textile (Fashion and Textiles). In a different city, these would be must-see attractions in their own right.

Money, Money, Money

The Cabinet des Médailles et Monnaies on rue de Richelieu has a slightly peculiar collection of exhibits, including a vast hoard of coins, medals and tokens – over half a million in all. There's also a range of antiques, including silverware, jewellery and the 7th century Dagobert's Throne, on which French kings were once crowned. This is the oldest museum in France and in the afternoon, it's freeee.

Rue Montorgueil – Food Heaven

Lined with restaurants, cafés, bakeries, fish stores, cheese shops, wine shops, produce stands and flower shops, rue Montorgueil is a place for Parisians to socialize while doing their daily shopping. Nearby is Les Halles, containing the largest indoor (mostly underground) shopping mall in central Paris

Jardin due Palais Royal

The elegant Jardin du Palais Royal in summertime is a fine place to sit, muse and picnic. Key sights include the Cardinal Richelieu's Palais Royal itself (sorry, you can't visit) and Daniel Buren's candy-striped column artwork Les Deux Plateaux. Around the garden are three famous arcades: the Galerie de Valois (east), Galerie de Montpensier (west) and Galerie Beaujolais. The first of these is home to upmarket designer boutiques, whose prices appear ironic considering that the French revolution actually started in the second arcade.

Chapter 9
The Islands: 1st & 4th Arrondissements

17th		18th		19th	
		9th	10th	11th	20th
	8th	2nd	3rd		
16th		1st	4th	12th	
	7th	6th	5th	13th	
	15th	14th			

Right at Paris's historical epicentre on the river Seine float two tiny islands, Ile de la Cité and Ile St. Louis, packed with the remnants of their intriguing past. Like two pieces of fruit protected by an expanding shell, Paris's islands predate the arrondissements surrounding them: here you'll find Sainte-Chapelle, the only fragile remains of Ile de la Cité's old Palais de Justice still standing - and Place Dauphine, a secluded and beautiful square where the sounds of traffic ebb away to the gentle tap of a game of boules being played. Of course, the islands are dominated by the resplendent gothic masterpiece, Notre-Dame cathedral, rearing up from the Cité like a giant ship anchored with flying buttresses.

Headlines and highlights

- **Let the Lady of our Paris win your heart:** climb the towers of Cathedrale de Notre-Dame to get up close and personal with gargoyles and angels, and stand on Kilomètre zéro, at the symbolic heart of France

- **Embrace your avid reader, picnicker or petanque-player at Place Dauphine:** one of the prettiest squares in the City of Light has a centre of chestnut trees ideal to while away a peaceful afternoon

- **Explore the original streets of 19th century Ile de la Cité:** the only streets of the island remaining undestroyed by Baron Haussmann, Napoleon III's mayor of Paris, are to the north of the cathedral – rues Chanoinesse, des Ursins and de la Colombe

- **Marvel at the teetering turret of Sainte-Chapelle:** the fragile looking spire of Ile de la Cité's old palace is a testament to time, still standing tall despite its damage during the Revolution

- **Hang out at Paris's haunt for lovers, Ile St-Louis:** stroll around surveying elegant mansions and eating exquisite ice-cream.

Getting to the islands

The Île de la Cité is connected to the rest of Paris by bridges to both the left and right banks of the river Seine, and also to Île Saint-Louis. Île de la Cité also has a metro station (Cité), and if you're travelling from the suburbs, the RER station Saint-Michel-Notre-Dame on the Left Bank has an exit in front of the cathedral.

Cathédrale Notre Dame de Paris

This magnificent and world-famous piece of ecclesiastical architecture began construction in 1160 and was completed around 1345, then churning out six popes during the thirteenth and fourteenth centuries. During the Revolution, its ornaments suffered, with the entire frieze of Old Testament Kings being destroyed by people who mistook them for the Kings of France, and the steeple and gormless looking gargoyles added in their place: for a good close look, you can brave the ascent to the towers by climbing up through the side entrance to the cathedral, open April to September. You can also climb down into the crypt, 80 metres under the Notre Dame, built to protect the ruins discovered during excavations: entrance is available for free with a Paris Museum Pass - http://www.parispass.com/?ref=cj

Napoleon began to restore the building for his crowning here as emperor in 1804, but the real hard work was put in by Victor Hugo, who created a petition stirring public interest to amend the cathedral's sorry state in 1820. This project was particularly favored by the Romantic novelists of the city, who saw the gothic architectural elements as a great way to shelter tormented souls.

Today, the magnificent carvings on the building's facade tell stories of the Day of Judgement and the dead rising from their graves, Mary being crowned by Christ, and the Nativity scene, all heavy with symbolism and as visually arresting as myth would have the world believe.

What's better? Find yourself at a heavenly organ recital or Bach cantata at one of the world's most famous cathedrals.

Kilomètre zéro

Notre Dame might be the centre of the city, but it's also the symbolic centre of France. Exit the cathedral by the west door, and see the bronze star - Kilomètre zéro – from where all the main road distances in France are calculated.

Petanque at Place Dauphine

Shrouded by seventeenth century red brick houses, walk into Place Dauphine and find yourself in real island solitude, seemingly miles from the hum of traffic and city life. Created by Henri IV as a tribute to his son Louis XIII, the centre of the square (or in actual fact, triangle) is a park filled with chestnut trees, where Paris's citizens come to play a game of petanque or bocci balls – boules, as it's commonly known. Try a game, and they might even have some expert tips for you.

Ile St-Louis

There might not be much to tick off here in terms of sight-seeing, but roaming the Ile St-Louis is a real treat for lovers of architecture, just lovers, and historically convicts on the run from Paris's oldest prison, the Conciergerie. This small island counterpart was covered with swampy pastures, until the seventeenth century when developer Christophe Marie transformed it by building a series of majestic mansions – including the likes of Hotel Lauzun, home to poet Baudelaire for two years – and Hotel Lambert, some of which has been sadly destroyed by fire but is still widely considered to be one of the most beautiful residences in Paris. A visit to the island wouldn't be complete without a stroll to the southern quais, where you can visit Berthillon for one of its incredible ice creams: wander down St-Louis-en-l'Ile attached to your other half and soak up the atmosphere at sunset.

17th		18th		19th	
		9th	10th	11th	20th
	8th	2nd	3rd		
16th		1st	4th	12th	
	7th	6th	5th	13th	
	15th	14th			

Artsy, and preserved in equal measures of sophistication and antiquity, this is a part of Paris which wasn't rebuilt – or destroyed – by Haussmann in the 19th century. Rather than grand boulevards and open spaces, Le Marais is all twisting streets as it was 200 years ago, winding maze-like between an outcrop of cool bars and restaurants, and emerging designer boutiques. Le Marais means 'swamp', which it was until the 13th century, after which it developed into the poshest neighborhood in Paris, home to aristocracy and their grand residences – and is now home to a thriving gay scene and Jewish community, all squashed into an affluent warren of culturally important monuments and museums.

- Spend hours trawling the Pompidou Centre, through reams of multi-disciplinary modern art

Find a more intimate art experience at Musée Cognacq-Jay, and an artist insight at the Musée Picasso

- Discover Marché des Enfants Rouges, the oldest covered market of Paris

- Be blown away by the aristocratic magnificence of Place des Vosges and its formal garden

- Trace the history of Paris right from its origins through Musée Carnavalet

- Seize Le Marais's mix of shopping opportunities, from boutique stores in secluded squares, to farmers' markets

- People-watch on the Rue de Francs-Bourgeois, the "street of the outspoken middle classes"

Pompidou Centre

Though this world-class art gallery attracting millions of visitors every year is a resounding success now, it wasn't always so popular: with its stripped down infrastructure bearing the bones and entrails of the building, giving it a crazed snakes and ladders appearance, critics scoffed at its radical form. Now, former Prime Minister Georges Pompidou can rest in his grave, his vision of the gallery's artistic integrity a reality. The centre's largest and most impressive collection is considered to be its modern art museum, the largest in Europe with an excess of 65,000 works which need to be rotated. For those who are somehow nonplussed by the collection of art, ascend the transparent escalator on the outside of the building, scan across panoramic views of the city... and then go back down and do it again.

Place des Vosges

Nothing quite prepares you for the grandeur of this square, lined with pink bricked architecture and stone mansions. The oldest square in Paris, it is seen as one of the first shining examples of public aristocratic elegance, commissioned in 1605 by Henri IV and then used as a venue for a royal wedding - the chestnut trees in the central gardens shrouding a statue of Louis XIII, who married Anne of Austria here. Today, you'll find upmarket art, fashion and antique shops lining its edges, with buskers making the area ring with the sounds of classical music and jazz.

Musée Carnavalet

Charting your way through the city's history all the way through to the Belle Époque, the era of peace and optimism before World War I began, this is an extraordinary journey through paintings, sculptures, architectural relics and decorative elements, all pulling together Paris's story. The greatest thing about this museum is perhaps that it's rarely crowded in comparison to Paris's other huge cultural centres – but please, don't quote us on it.

Musée Cognacq-Jay

Just one block west from Musée Carnavalet, this gallery sits inside one of the area's impressive Hôtel de Donon. This was once the residence of Théodore-Ernest Cognacq and his wife Marie-Louise Jay, who were department store owners, philanthropists and noted lovers of eighteenth century European art: this intimate and impressive collection remains.

Marché des Enfants Rouges

Buried away behind an inconspicuous looking green metal gate, the oldest covered market in Paris is a trove of ready-to-eat food stalls which, if you can't find the market in the first place, will entice you there anyway with an array of mouth watering aromas wafting to your nostrils from all over the globe. Come for a meander and a munch with the locals.

Rue de Francs-Bourgeois

The main lateral street on the northern part of the Marais, writer Jack Kerouac gave this narrow, culturally eye-opening stretch his own translation of "the street of the outspoken middle classes": whilst an accurate portrayal of its contemporary populace, the name actually refers to "people exempt from tax", which stems from the "Chez Ma Tante" pawn shop at no.55, otherwise known as municipal credit, a public institution which lends cash in exchange for items such as jewellery or works of art. Since it is generally seen as embarrassing to borrow money by French society, the institution took its name from the expression "we got some money from my aunt."

Musée Picasso

On the northern side of rue-des Francs Bourgeois, rue Payenne leads onto Parc-Royal and arrives at no.5 rue de Thorigny, where you'll find another Hôtel concealing a renovated Picasso exhibition, which has grown exponentially in size and now represents almost every significant period in the artist's life, an excellent tribute to his development, difficulties and personal insight through paintings.

17th		18th		19th	
8th	9th	10th	11th		20th
	2nd	3rd			
16th	8th	1st	4th	12th	
	7th	6th	5th	13th	
	15th	14th			

Originally full of clergymen and university scholars milling around the area's many medieval colleges, this Quarter takes its descriptive name from their commonly spoken language. This area, still steeped in medieval antiquity, remains an academic area and is home to some of France's most stellar educational institutes, including the famous Sarbonne and Jussieu campuses. The name alone evokes images of Paris at its bohemian height, and although the Latin Quarter's gentrified postcodes mean that students usually can't afford the rent these days, there is still a seductive selection of cheaper bars, cafes and bistros which resurrect that electric sense of change you can feel when reading the works of Sartre, Camus and Beckett.

Headlines and highlights

- Duck inside the great hulk of The Pantheon to appreciate this landmark to France's greatest heroes and heroines

- Sit outside a cafe and watch student tote their books about at The University quarter, and the huddle of arty cinemas at top creative institution, the Sorbonne

- Breathe easy in Paris's most gorgeous green spaces at Jardin des Plantes, Jardin Alpin & Jardin Ecologique

- Take a peaceful walk and grab some lunch down Rue Mouffetard, taking advantage of the traces of this former great market street of Paris

- Marvel at the best preserved Roman remains in all Paris, including third century baths at Musée National du Moyen Age

Gardens of the Latin Quarter

Roam around Jardin des Plantes: combining the appeal of a local park with a botanical haven, you can grab an ice cream and climb up the labyrinth to the belvedere here, and also appreciate the science behind the shrubbery. From tropical greenhouses to medicinal plant displays, this is a fascinating place of discovery devoted to the eco systems of the Ile de France. To the north of the Plantes lies Jardin Alpin, a sheltered, sunken place filled with mountain plants from all over the world. Peek through the fence at Jardin Ecologique, which was cordoned off into its own gem-like preserve decades ago, but crams in the natural flora of the Parisian basin, somehow stuffed with miniature wildflower meadows. Blooming lovely.

The Pantheon

A former church dedicated to St. Genevieve and her relics, this great hulk of a dome squatting on this neo-classical facade houses the remains of a long list of very important French people, including Voltaire, Rousseau, Hugo and more recently, Marie Curie, who are entombed in the vast crypt below.

The University quarter

Wander down the studious Rue des Ecoles, which marks the beginning of the University quarter. Rub the toe of the great Renaissance academic, Michel de Montaigne for luck, which you'll find has already been dulled by the thumbs of many students seeking some Dutch, or French courage before their exams over generations. Turn down rue Champollion, and take your pick of the street's arty cinemas before finding yourself at place de la Sorbonne, and kill some hours sitting outside a cafe under the lime trees, witnessing the buzz among a future generation of creatives and admiring the Chapelle Ste-Ursule, a 1640 building which established a trend for a skyline of Roman reformation domes punctuating the Parisian skyline.

Rue Mouffetard

George Orwell's description of "La Mouffe" as a "ravine of tall, leprous houses" is only true around the top half around the rue de Pot de Fer, which has been given over to tacky eating places. At the southern end, however, you can find the trappings of the street's tradition as a great market street, with excellent cheese and wine shops, and a clutch of authentic market cafes. Gaze up at St Médard, opposite the beautiful painted facade at no.134 rue Mouffetard, once a country Parish church. It was sacked by Protestant rioters back in 1561, and was the site of many self-sacrificing 'convulsionnaires' in 1727, who gathered at the grave of Francois de Paris – hysterical, eating the earth, and sometimes even crucifying themselves.

Musée National du Moyen Age

Worth visiting if not only for the incredible tapestry series and a widely noted masterpiece of European art, The Lady and the Unicorn, this treasure trove of Roman relics is housed behind the grand walls of what was formerly hôtel de Cluny. If medieval music concerts take your fancy, the "heure musicale" is worth the six euros. After the Cluny on the walk up St. Michel, you'll generally find less crowded and more authentic cafes, and quality second hand bookstores to browse through, a hotbed for students searching for cheap deals on their required reading materials.

Chapter 12
Saint-Germain-des-Prés, the literary heart of Paris: 6th Arrondissement

17th		18th		19th
16th	8th	9th	10th	11th	20th
		2nd	3rd		
		1st	4th	12th	
	7th	6th	5th	13th	
	15th	14th			

Covering the 6e arrondissement up to the eastern fringe of 7e, turn the pages of this storied neighbourhood, its past enriched with existential meet-ups, inspired artists, and jazz masters haunting the late night dive bars. Despite the fact that J.P Sartre's ghost keeping office hours in the local cafes is now a distant blur, St. Germain is still blessed with a youthful energy, fascinating streets to explore and the atmosphere of a university district spilling over from the Latin Quarter. Less gritty than it was, Parisians clinging to tradition may avert their eyes at the district's emergent Pseudo-culture – and tradition may have taken a back seat here – but it's hardly turned into a home for philistinism, and the inevitable renewal of tradition is what makes the area so interesting. It's virtually impossible to be disappointed by the boutique hotels, high end art galleries, design shops, bookstores, churches and sprawling parklands of St. Germain.

Headlines and highlights

- Discuss surrealism over an expresso in Picasso's favourite Café de Flore, or contemplate the futility of existence and put pen to paper in Deux Magots, frequented by Sartre, Hemmingway and Simone de Beauvoir

- Make like Hemingway and shoot down or strangle some pigeons for your dinner in Jardin du Luxembourg*, or for the conventional sightseeing tourist, enjoy the outdoor cinema in summer and take a stroll to admire the sculptures

- Take a stroll down rue Bonaparte to find the Ecole des Beaux Arts, which many of art history's greats passed through before anyone knew them

- Ignore the throng of tourists and make your way down rue Buci onto rue St. Andre des Arts, a lively street filled with all of Paris's edible and alcoholic indulgence

- Behold the obligatory church, Saint-Germain-des-Prés, a powerful tower dominating the place where French philosopher René Descartes, among others, is buried

- As you approach the 7e arrondissement, be electrified by a visit to Musée d'Orsay, its collection of Impressionist and post-Impressionist works making it one of Paris's most visited attractions

Jardin du Luxembourg

*Ernest Hemingway claimed that when he was struggling for money, he would often take refuge in the vast landscapes of the park and strange the odd pigeon, hiding it in his son's pram to provide food for the family.

A whole sixty acres of park in the middle of the city, Jardin du Luxembourg is the heart – and the lungs of Paris. After a multitudinous shopping experience in St. Germain, you will appreciate the escape. Find a chair by the main fountain and lounge in the sun, or head to the south east where it's more private, admire the closely manicured flowerbeds and detailed aesthetics of the gardens, and wend your way around scattered sculptures, ranging from the historic, to the bizarre, to a miniature Statue of Liberty. If you are a kid, have kids or are relatively small, there are ponies and donkeys to rent for a ride around the gardens.

Rue Bonaparte

Less visible than the Boulevard St. Germain but just as intellectually authentic, continue down rue Bonaparte for a while and see Ecole des Beaux Arts on your left. At the turn of the century, this institution notorious for its prestige and traditional training methods was where the greats learned the tricks they later decided to break: Moreau, Degas, Monet, and Renoir are just a few household names which might make your ears prick. If that's not enough to sate your hunger for arty atmosphere, turn right at rue de Seine for high end art galleries specialising in 19th and 20th century prints and masters.

Rue St. Andre des Arts

If it wasn't already obvious enough, it's unlikely that you will leave St. Germain without over-indulging – whether eating too much, getting drunk, or both. The renowned Café Le Procope is just a right turn down rue de l'Ancienne Comédie, founded in 1686 and reputedly the oldest cafe/restaurant in France. A long list of French philosophy's names also dined here – including Voltaire – who might have been impressed by the stunning interior, or simply the fact that it doesn't look like a Catholic church.

Musée d'Orsay

On this side of St. Germain swinging up towards the river is Musée d'Orsay, facing the Tuileries gardens to the west across on the opposite bank. There's more to it than just Renoir and Monet, although they in themselves are probably enough to pore over. From the ground floor displaying a series of serious-minded artworks from the 19th century, to the Impressionists' gallery, with oriental art and impressive large-format paintings in between, this is a delicious art sandwich to get your teeth into.

17th		18th		19th	
		9th	10th	11th	20th
	8th	2nd	3rd		
16th		1st	4th	12th	
	7th	6th	5th	13th	
	15th	14th			

This vast iron lattice straddling a bend in the Seine happily surveys one of Paris's most relentlessly walkable, edible, pretty and visitor-friendly districts. You may have turned to this section of the guide first, and this is your lucky day, apart from the obvious monumental reason: the Eiffel Tower quarter is a showcase of worldwide city design, with vistas planned for sheer magnificence – from the marble neoclassical monster of the Palais de Chaillot to the most ornate bridge in the city, Pont Alexandre III, which despite its beauty was still subject to strict controls not to obscure the views of the surrounding Champs-Élysées or the Invalides.

Headlines and highlights

- Scale the quintessential symbol of Paris, the Eiffel Tower, which was supposed to be a temporary structure for a fair

- Hungry? Roam Rue Cler, a food lover's paradise filled with edible goods you can only find in France

- The brash Musée du Quai Branly cuts a postmodern swathe - and it's great. Visit this relative newcomer on the museum scene for contemporary art and unbeatable views

- Don't miss the tomb of Napoleon in the crushingly grand Eglise du Dome, Invalides quarter

- Admire the works of one of the world's greatest sculptors in the prettiest setting at Musée Rodin

- The bridge of Pont Alexandre III all but parades across the Seine, its name and elaborate decoration symbolising Franco-Russian friendship

Eiffel Tower and around

As a visitor, you can't go to Paris and not see the Eiffel Tower, mainly because you can see it from all over the city. The towering ode to industrial engineering was built especially to commemorate the 100th anniversary of the French Revolution - a grand scale capitalist extravaganza which was only meant to last for 20 years. At 300m, it was the tallest building ever built at the time, and not receiving the desired reaction, critics described it as a "grimy factory chimney" and a "grotesque mercantile imagining". Gustave Eiffel argued that it was a perfect piece of utilitarian architecture.

Got a head for heights? If the elevation frightens you, the queues are even scarier: they are likely to be l – o – n – g. Paris looks surreally microscopic from up there, and the views are probably better from the second level, especially on hazy or cloudier days. After those dizzying altitudes, head to the Champ de Mars just back from the Eiffel Tower, a popular spot for sunbathing in summer which was a venue for the city's great revolutionary fairs.

Take a step back after sunset, when the Eiffel Tower is bathed with a golden glow, and a light show ignites the structure every hour on the hour.

An autumnal eiffel tower

Invalides quarter

This area was built for retired or wounded soldiers in the reign of Louis XIV, hence its name. The main sight here is the resplendent guilded dome of Hotel des Invalides, a decadent shell for the Army museum and the tomb of Napoleon. The Eglise du Dome, has a separate entrance on the south side of the complex: if the architecture was decadent, Napoleon's resting place pulls out all the stops – a mighty deep red sarcophagus in a circular pit, overlooked by guardian soldier statues and surrounded by relics of military victory.

Rue Cler

Between the Invalides, rue Cler doesn't scream grand austerity like the rest of the district, but offers a distinctly posh culinary experience for a treat: this market street houses permanent delicatessens, fruit stalls on barrows, and the surrounding area offers classy boutiques, bistros and little hotels.

Musée Rodin

This mansion with a generous outcrop of garden is another lovely setting for a museum in Paris – and perhaps one of the loveliest. Leased from the state by the sculptor himself, Rodin promised in return to gift all of his work to the government following his death. The passionate intensity of the sculptures is hauntingly felt throughout the museum, often crowded with visitors eager to see works like The Kiss, with Paolo, the subject's ecstatically scrunched up toes. Head outside among the grounds for bronze works, one of which – The Gate of Hell – forms the centrepiece of the garden pond.

La Pagode

Originally built as a present for the wife of a director of the Bonmarché department store, the Chinese-style roofs of La Pagode were later turned into a historic cinema, the first to screen the movies of the Nouvelle Vague. It was renovated, and today it remains one of the best art-house cinemas in the city both visually, with its Oriental-meets-art-deco décor - and in terms of cinematic content.

Chapter 14
The Champs Elysées: 8th Arrondissement

17th		18th		19th	
	8th	9th	10th	11th	20th
16th		2nd	3rd		
		1st	4th	12th	
	7th	6th	5th	13th	
	15th	14th			

Welcome to the Champs Elysées and welcome to the good life and the glamour, where you can walk down the most famous avenue in the world. This is the real life manifestation of silver screen Paris – the city of myth and films. Here in this exclusive district, you'll find luxury hotels, top fashion boutiques, monuments and symmetrical landscaping: Champs Elysées even means 'Elysian Fields', a patch of heaven on earth. Despite its name, though, it's the history of the place which really holds it together – once the famed meeting place for politicians and intellectuals, Paris's biggest shopping district has caved to make way for commercialism and a new age crassness – but squint, stroll the massive pavements with their elegant facades and leafy trees – and be taken back to another era.

Headlines and highlights

- Stroll through Elysian Fields (Champs Elysées), which despite the chain stores, is beginning to retain something of its former cachet

- Take a sobering backward glance at Musée Nissim De Camond, a private home once owned by a wealthy Parisian family murdered by Nazis

- Peruse the works at the Petit Palais: Musée des Beaux-Arts, hardly 'petit' but certainly palatial

- Gawk past Place de la Concorde, providing the quintessential Parisian view of all the city's grand landmarks

- Wander down Avenue de Wagram from place de l'Etoile and feed your senses with the flower market, cafes and brightly coloured Art Nouveau ceramics

Champs Elysées – a brief history

You might not want to spend too much time on this avenue radiating out from place de l'Etoile, but it's a definite must for first-time visitors. Beginning life as a leafy promenade extending from the Tuileries gardens, high society lined it with lavish mansions and the elite of Paris frequented the area's cafes and theatres. Now, it's been tarnished by the hand of capitalism, but remnants of the avenue remain: visit Lido cabaret, Fouquet's cafe-restaurant, the perfumier Guerlain's shop, and the former Claridges hotel (which is now a shopping arcade) to build an image of Champs Elysées in its former romantic glory.

Petit Palais

Facing the Grand Palais with its 45m cupola which can be seen from most of the city's viewpoints, the Petit Palais is only comparatively small, and no less highly decorated: an interior garden, beautiful spiral staircase and grand gallery akin to Versailles' Hall of Mirrors make this establishment a feature in itself, but it's the Musée des Beaux-Arts de la Ville de Paris's clutch of creative treasures crossing epochs which make the place really special. Across two floors and ranging from ancient Greek and Roman, through to the early 20th century, it kind of looks like it has mopped up the remnants left behind by Paris's other noteable galleries – but treasures by Monet, Courbet and Pissarro, along with a whimsical collection of furniture and jewellery, make Musée des Beaux-Arts fascinating in its own right.

Musée Nissim De Camondo

A homely (albeit over-the-top homely) mixture of 18th century decorative art and painting, this collection was built up by Count de Camondo, the son of a wealthy Sephardic Jewish banker who immigrated from Istanbul to Paris in the late 19th century. The Count commissioned a period mansion to display all of his relics, and now you can wander around rooms overflowing with tapestries, pastoral scenes, and gilded furniture. Then there are the homelier upper floors, where the family spent their time. The remnants of individual taste and empty personal spaces become tinged with melancholia as you learn about the Camondos and their fate: the Count's wife left him for the head groom, his son Nissim, after whom the museum is named, died on a World War I flying mission, whilst his remaining daughter perished with her children in the camps of World War II.

Place de la Concorde

Get ready to frame your photo: from here you can see the Arc de Triomphe in the distance, the massive avenue stretching towards it, the Madeleine church, Hotel de Crillon, the Grand Palais, and the Eiffel tower soaring above it all. All testaments to Parisian history, the city does not forget those executed in the square during the revolution, including Louis XVI and Marie-Antoinette. It's worth taking a walk straight towards the Arc in the evening when the lights are on, or at Christmas, when thousands twinkle in the giant trees like a layer of festive fairy dust.

Avenue de Wagram

An interesting, comparatively suburban diversion to the Champs Elysées, you can pause to enjoy the Art Nouveau facade at no.34, which is now a slightly faded set of swirly lines and bright ceramics, but caused some controversy back at the beginning of the 20th century. Further on, you will arrive at place des Ternes, with its flower market and cafes. Turn down Ternes to savour the sights and aromas of rue Poncelet street market, with local butchers, grocers and fishmongers' stalls interjected with some very fine food shops too tempting to ignore; especially Alléosse, which is probably the best cheesemonger in Paris.

Chapter 15

Opera Garnier to the foot of Montmartre: 9th arrondissement

17th		18th		19th	
	8th	9th	10th	11th	20th
16th		2nd	3rd		
		1st	4th	12th	
	7th	6th	5th	13th	
	15th	14th			

Developed during the Belle-Epoche era of the early 1900s, this arrondissement on the Right Bank of the Seine encompassing the Opera Garnier, Grand Magasins and Grands Boulevards straddles a diverse and likeable middle ground between historic grandeur and a fading red light district. High-end boutiques, resplendent covered walkways, or galleries, flagship department stories and the original Opera in the southern part of the district provide a distinctly different atmosphere to South Pigalle, or 'SoPi' as it's referred to affectionately, mainly by the resident hipsters. This northern neighbourhood of the 9th arrondissement, which closely adjoins Montmartre, offers a growing culture of bourgeois bohemia (BoBo – another locally coined abbreviation) as a slew of stylish restaurants, bars and budget shops open up in the area. Clubs and theatres here have reeled in pleasure-seekers for centuries, so jump in and enjoy.

Headlines and highlights

- The wide pavements of the Grands Boulevards are ideal for a spot of people-watching, nursing cafés crèmes and browsing the 19th century arcades

- Don't miss the ballet, or a less frequent opera at Palais Garnier, a memorable and grand way to experience one of Paris's symbolic cultural cornerstones

- An essential stop for fashion enthusiasts, Galeries Lafayette Department Store is near the stately Opera and sings "Belle-Epoche" just as well with cutting edge designer collections

- Be bowled over by bustling South Pigalle for stylish cocktail bars and clubs – with its official stamp of cool but yet still ripe for discovery (see below and Montmartre: 18th arrondissement)

- Have your heart won by Musée de la Vie Romantique in New Athens, South Pigalle, with its harmonious historical setting and relics.

Grands Boulevards

During the Belle Epoche, the Grands Boulevards were the place to be seen. Still today, you can soak up the atmosphere of these architectural gems by wandering through the ornate passages couverts, glass-roofed arcades that served as the forerunners world's first malls, and finding your gaze peeled towards the windows of over-priced shops. Find Gallerie Vivienne, a contender for the prettiest, and for a lengthy stroll into centuries past, Passage Jouffroy leading onto Passage Verdeau. Back in 18th or 19th century Paris, these passageways would allow people to take shortcuts, shelter from the rain, shop, dine, wander aimlessly and admire, or spend a secluded hour in the arms of a lover.

These boulevards join the Arc de Triomphe, place de la Concorde, place de la Madeleine and the Opera – and are all lined with Haussmann-era buildings. For any fans of haute couture, you might find yourself spending some big euros here. For anyone who enjoys nothing more than a good rummage in a charity shop, you can use the experience as an education in French high fashion – especially when visiting the grands magasins (department stores) like Le Printemps and Galeries Lafayette, entrenched in the luxury of former glory days.

Palais Garnier

If you're not planning on seeing an Opera, then the Palais Garnier is definitely worth a visit anyway. This monument has provided more artistic inspiration than most others in the city: approach the place and see music and dance sculptures on the facade, Apollo on the copper dome, and nymphs bearing torches.

Venture inside and you'll find Degas' ballerinas, Chagall's ceiling, and Gaston Leroux's Phantom, offering layers upon layers of drama and intrigue to

Haussmann's grandiose urban renovation project. Make sure you don't miss the Grand Staircase, the library museum on the first floor and the horse-shoe shaped auditorium on the second floor – with its gilded interior and red velvet seats.

The Ballet de l'Opéra National de Paris successfully treads between classics and new productions – toeing the line somewhere between Opera Bastille and the lavish Palais Garnier.

Musée de la Vie Romantique

Musée de la Vie Romantique is a villa located in the neighbourhood of New Athens, built by Dutch artist Ary Scheffer in 1830. Here, you can soak up the relics of the Romantic era and spend time at the café and cute garden in an area which once teemed with writers, artists and composers - the perfect garden for a lazy afternoon. It's hard to put a finger on what's so special about the museum's adjoining rose garden come tea room, with its floral wallpaper and greenhouse ceiling, and the gardens, fringed with fuchsias. It might be that despite everyone knowing about the place, it makes you feel like you've found one of Paris's closely guarded secrets - a slice of peace which is far removed from the pace of the city for a bit of respite.

Pay attention to SoPi

...You'll be using the local term in no time. Pay attention to the often overlooked New Athens (above) which is filled with neoclassical mansions by creatives in the 19th century. Wander down Rue Ballu, Rue St Lazare, Rue de la Tour-des-Dames and Rue de la Rochefoucauld to fully appreciate their magnificence.

Places to go in Pigalle

Pigalle has a historical reputation for sleaze, peep shows and sex shops, but this seediness is giving way to a new emerging culture of young, wholesome bohemia. You'll find plenty of folks lining the pavements outside cool music venues such as Boule Noir, La Cigale and La Machine du Moulin Rouge – a hotbed of electro next door to the Moulin Rouge cabaret.

Chapter 16

Les Gares & Bastille 10th 11th 12th Arrondissements

17th		18th		19th	
		9th	10th	11th	20th
	8th	2nd	3rd		
16th		1st	4th	12th	
	7th	6th	5th	13th	
	15th	14th			

These three arrondissements are often a low-priority destination for visitors... and that's a shame, because there's a lot to see in these large residential areas of Paris, which contain the great 'gares' – the wonderfully designed railway stations which serve the city.

The 10th in particular is an up-and-coming neighbourhood: young, hip and trend-setting. It hosts Canal Saint-Martin, which connects the waterways north-east of Paris to the Seine. These are traditionally working-class areas, with a history of radical and revolutionary activity, and these days Bastille and the districts further east, are some of the most diverse and vibrant parts of the city, home to sizeable ethnic populations, as well as students and artists, guaranteeing a fine selection of bars, restaurants, and night-life.

Headlines and Highlights

Canal St-Martin

The southern part of the Canal St-Martin is charming in all seasons, with elegant plane trees lining the cobbled quais, and high-arched footbridges separating the locks. Lining this stretch are loads of lovely and lively bars, cafés, bistros and boutiques; much- patronised by cool, artistic folk like us. The canal has been made famous in art (Sisley), song (Piaf) and film (Amelie). This is a great place to walk, cycle or just laze on a tour boat. On most Sundays the quais are closed to traffic, and in summer people routinely come to just hang out along the canal's edge and on the café terraces.

Alongside the canal is one of Paris's architectural masterpieces: the early seventeenth-century Hôpital St-Louis. This still operates as a hospital (excuse the pun), but a visitor can explore its calm central courtyard and admire the elegant façades and steep-pitched roofs that once sheltered the city's plague victims.

At the southern end, the canal goes underground, and a wide boulevard follows its course: attractively landscaped and hosting an excellent food market on Thursdays an Saturday mornings.

Bastille

The word 'Bastille' can refer to an area of Paris, to one specific square (Place de la Bastille), or of course to the prison famously stormed in 1789. This paragraph directly relates to the Place de la Bastille – and its opera - but the whole quarter is worth exploring. This used to be a working-class district in spirit and in style, but is now notable for its trendy shops and energetic night-life, especially on rue de Lappe.

Place de la Bastille itself is a big busy square, dominated by the Opéra Bastille and to a lesser extent by the column which commemorates 14 July 1789, when the Bastille prison fortress was stormed, triggering the French Revolution and the end of feudalism in Europe. The opera offers a full and varied programme and tickets can be booked online.

Promenade Plantée

Variously known as the Coulée verte René-Dumont or Promenade plantée (tree-lined walkway) or just Coulée verte (green course), this lovely urban feature is a 4.7 km elevated linear park built on top of obsolete railway infrastructure, offering a wonderful country walk in the middle of the city. One section, the Viaduc des arts, is – as you might guess – a viaduct on which the old railway buildings have been converted into a string of art galleries and craft workshops, with a couple of cafés.

Other places to go and see

Bercy

The Parc de Bercy is a public park sited on what-used-to-be a large complex of wine warehouses. The park is made up of three different gardens on different themes connected by foot bridges. The Cinémathèque Française designed by Frank Gehry, is also in the park, and on the raised terraces are the 21 sculptures of Rachid Khimoune's 'Children of the World'. The park is linked directly to the National Library of France by the Simone de Beauvoir footbridge over the Seine. The Musée des Arts Forains is also located here, offering displays of funfair art and equipment.

The Great Gares

Three of Paris's six railway stations are in this area: Gare du Nord, Gare, Gare de l'Est and Gare de Lyon. All three offer superb examples of 19th century French industrial architecture. Gare du Nord is the busiest station in Europe, and has featured in a host of films and books, from The Bourne Identity to The Da Vinci Code. Gare de l'Est is slightly older, and just as architecturally interesting. Both stations have fine examples of 19th century memorial statuary.

Cirque d'Hiver

The Cirque d'Hiver (Winter Circus) has in its time been a prominent venue for circuses, dressage, concerts, Turkish wrestling and fashion shows. These days, while you can visit the building and photograph its grandeur any time, the best time to head to Cirque d'Hiver is in January when it plays host to the combined Festival Mondial du Cirque de Demain and Festival Mondial du Cirque de l'Avenir; showcasing modern circus acts and new circus stars from around the world.

Great Museums of Not-a-Great-Deal

This area offers two excellent small museums, each focusing in depth, almost obsessively, on one topic. The Musée de l'Éventail is without question the best museum in Paris dealing exclusively with fans (not electric fans; the kind that ladies wave at the opera). The Musée du Fumeur (smoking) contains clay pipes, peace pipes, hookahs, Chinese opium pipes, Egyptian sheeshas, and snuffboxes, as well as cigars, tobacco samples, hemp-fibre clothing, and etchings; plus portraits, photographs, videos, and scientific drawings; all without really explaining why people aren't satisfied with good old fresh air.

Passage Brady

Passage Brady is a long iron-and-glass covered arcade, with stalls and small shops along its length. Its particular claim to fame is that it houses the best collection of

Indian, Pakistani and Bangladeshi restaurants in France – reasonably priced, and really good.

Bois de Vincennes

The Bois de Vincennes is the largest public park in the city. It contains the Château de Vincennes, a former residence of the Kings of France; an English landscape garden with four lakes; a zoo; an arboreteum; a floral garden; a horse-racing track; and a velodrome for bicycle races. For most people, though, it is just a nice place to relax.

17th		18th		19th	
	8th	9th	10th	11th	20th
		2nd	3rd		
16th		1st	4th	12th	
	7th	6th	5th	13th	
	15th	14th			

The south of Paris has one great attraction for the tourist: an almost-complete absence of other tourists. These large residential arrondissements sprawl along what used-to-be the line of the last defensive wall surrounding Paris, and nowadays follow the line of the Paris ring road, the Périphérique. Compared to the centre, there isn't a huge amount to see, but there is plenty of history in these streets, especially if you are an art-lover. Montparnasse became the artistic haunt-of-choice for the bohemian crew following World War I, and as you sip a coffee on Rue Vavin, consider that these pavements were walked by Chagall, Giacometti, Kandinsky, Matisse, Modigliani, and Picasso... oh, and not to forget our transatlantic visitors: Man Ray, Ezra Pound and Ernest Hemingway. This is, to many people, the 'real' Paris, packed with excellent bistros, cafés, and brasseries.

OK, there aren't that many must-see attractions here – but go anyway. When you visit a city like Paris, packed to the brim with iconic sights and locations, it is tempting to tick off the top ten and take a well-deserved rest. Fair enough, but most experienced travellers would advise against spending all of your stay in the time-honoured tourist-traps. If you do, you'll probably not gain much understanding of the city, and you'll certainly miss out on some great experiences. By all means have a coffee and croissant in a café next to the Eiffel Tower, but the coffee and pastries are wonderful everywhere, and they'll be even friendlier and much cheaper if you explore towards the edge of town.

Headlines and Highlights

The Catacombs

This underground warren of tunnels was formed from the quarries which used to be worked under Paris – a vast network, over 300Km in all. When the quarries closed, a creative use was found for the tunnels: to address a lack of space in the cities graveyards. Between 1785 and 1865 the rocky corridors were gradually filled with around six million skeletal remains, heaped higgledy-piggledy alongside the walkway. Obviously, this is not a visit to interest everyone, but older children seem to love a gruesome break from art galleries.

Note 1: You might guess that it gets hot and dry in these narrow tunnels, especially as there is a 2Km walk involved. Wrong: it's distinctly cool, and sometimes muddy under-foot. Dress sensibly.

Note 2: The comment earlier about 'an absence of tourists' does not apply to the catacombs. You need to get here early to avoid long queues. Ideally, turn up an hour before opening: there's plenty of places nearby for a take-away coffee and a pastry.

Note 3: If your ghoulish hike gives you an appetite, there's an excellent food market, and cafés on rue Daguerre, just round the corner.

Other places to go and see

Chinatown

The biggest 'Chinatown' in Europe is not actually very Chinese. It was originally almost entirely Vietnamese in culture, but now also comprises Cambodian, Thai and Laotian communities – as well as Chinese. Obviously, restaurants and food shops attract the visitor, but there are concerts of Chinese music on most weekday afternoons, and a pleasant park nearby.

Bibliothèque Nationale

This is one of Paris's outstanding pieces of modern architecture. The national library is clearly of limited interest if you don't read French, but it also offers the homesick an extremely comprehensive selection of foreign newspapers to browse. There are also regular, high quality exhibitions on literary themes, but the real star of the show is the building itself – the four huge L-shaped towers are intended to look like open books...

Montparnasse Tower

This brown glass monolith – a 59-floor office block with a café and observation deck near the top – highlights an interesting paradox regarding sight-seeing: why would you queue to climb the Eiffel Tower and gaze on this ugly building, when you could sip a coffee here and gaze across at spectacular views of the Eiffel Tower?

Montparnasse Cemetery

This high-walled cemetery is nicely located, with a daily food market and good cafés nearby. On Sundays there is also an excellent craft-market, with potters, painters and personalities to peer at. The cemetery is a pleasant place for a stroll, with several oddities of nineteenth century necropolis-art to see. Famous residents include Jean-Paul Sartre and Simone de Beauvoir (together, of course) and singer Serge Gainsbourg. Monsieur Gainsbourg's tomb is still visited regularly by fans, who may leave letters, cigarettes and gifts.

17th		18th		19th	
		9th	10th	11th	20th
	8th	2nd	3rd		
		1st	4th	12th	
16th	7th	6th	5th	13th	
	15th	14th			

The wealthy suburban areas of Paris are in the large arrondissements on the west side of the city. The 16th is one of the poshest of Parisian places-to-live. There is not a lot for a tourist to see, but in the enclave of narrow streets you can find some of the best luxury food shopping in Paris.

The Suburbs:

There is some linguistic confusion over the word 'suburban'. The French word for suburb is 'banlieue' and it really means something different. The 'suburbs' in the UK and US imply dull middle-class gentility and respectability. In Paris, 'banlieues' imply something a lot more edgy: a suggestion of socialism, ethnic diversity, teenage rebellion; tower blocks, spicy food and loud hip-hop music. 'Banlieues' are also explicitly outside the city boundaries. So, just to be clear: the 16th and 17th arrondissements are definitely suburbs of the 'leafy gentility' variety.

Headlines and highlights

Arc de Triomphe

At the boundary of the 16th, 17th and 8th arrondissements is the giant roundabout which holds one of Paris's most iconic sights: the Arc de Triomphe. The structure is exactly what it says: a symbol of, and memorial to, various military victories, begun by Napoleon, and completed by others. Poignantly, of course, Prussian and German armies have posed and preened in front of it, and its symbolism is less potent these days. It is, though, still very visit-able, and the views at dusk on a sunny are worth the 280-step climb.

The Musée Marmottan

The Musée Marmottan is notable for its fabulous collection of Monet paintings, bequeathed to the museum by the artist's son. Among them is Impression, an 1872 depiction of a misty Le Havre which gave the Impressionist movement its name. There are also world-class examples of increasingly abstract canvases from Monet's last years at Giverny. The museum collection also includes some of Monet's contemporaries, both famous and should-be-famous: Manet, Renoir and Berthe Morisot.

Other places to go and see

The Palais de Chaillot

Architecturally, it's pretty horrible: adorned with a 1937 blend of modernism and neoclassical style. It is, though a nice place to view the Eiffel Tower, and it houses a number of different museums. In the south wing, there are two - the Musée de la Marine (Naval Museum) and the Musée de l'Homme (The Museum of Man). In the north wing, there's an architecture museum - the Cité de l'Architecture et du Patrimoine, and on the lower levels – for the younger visitor – an aquarium.

The Palais de Tokyo

The Palais de Tokyo was built in 1937 specifically to house museums of modern art, so its interior is flexible, spacious and ideally lit for the display of paintings. The east wing is home to the Musée d'Art Moderne de la Ville de Paris, the modern art museum of the city of Paris. The other wing is home to the Site de Création Contemporaine, which organizes temporary exhibits and events focused on contemporary art.

Guimet Museum

The Guimet Museum has one of the largest collections of Asian art outside Asia, and matches that quantity with quality. The covered courtyard offers a delightfully airy space in which to display the world-renowned collection of Khmer sculpture, and the rest of the museum employs dramatic lighting and imaginative displays to present its exotic collection of art.

Great Museums of Not-a-Great-Deal

This region of Paris is home to a number of tiny museums, which do not offer universal appeal, but are likely to delight those with a special interest. These include the Musée Baccarat (crystal glass), Musée Galliera (history of fashion), Musée de la Contrefaçon (counterfeiting), and of course we must not forget the Musée d'Art Dentaire (dental history).

Chapter 19
Montmartre: 18ᵗʰ Arrondissement

17ᵗʰ		18ᵗʰ		19ᵗʰ	
		9ᵗʰ	10ᵗʰ	11ᵗʰ	20ᵗʰ
	8ᵗʰ	2ⁿᵈ	3ʳᵈ		
16ᵗʰ		1ˢᵗ	4ᵗʰ	12ᵗʰ	
	7ᵗʰ	6ᵗʰ	5ᵗʰ	13ᵗʰ	
	15ᵗʰ	14ᵗʰ			

High up on the hill known as the Butte sits the former village of Montmartre, famous for its artists' studios and its nearby night life, where narrow streets twist and climb their way up to Sacre Coeur, the famous white church at the peak. Montmartre is definitely worth exploring on foot, but if hills aren't your thing, there is a funicular railway, and a Montmartrobus which tackle the slopes with ease. At night, there is plenty of life in the area, which has kept some of its artistic bohemianism, despite being one of Paris's chief tourist attractions. Nearby is the Moulin Rouge and the nightlife of the Pigalle.

Headlines and highlights

Sacré-Coeur Basilica

The highest point in Paris, the basilica steps offer fabulous views across the city. The church itself is – architecturally – a bit twee: an odd mixture of French and Byzantine architecture with a pimpled roof and nippled dome. One Parisian poet described it as 'like a big baby's bottle for the angels to suck'. Of course, this doesn't affect you if you are standing inside the dome, and this is exactly where you want to be: from here, the views are even better.

Pedestrian Pottering

For the physically fit, if the weather is good, simply wandering the cobblestoned streets of Montmartre, steeped in history and art, is one of the highlights of any trip to Paris. This is the Paris of myth and film: where

Picasso, Van Gogh, and Matisse worked, where the 1871 Paris Commune was established, and where the movies Amelie and Midnight in Paris were set. Just potter round and soak in the ambience. Look out for the Art Nouveau metro station at Abbesses, and the green cast-iron drinking fountains dotted around.

St-Ouen Market

Strictly speaking, St-Ouen market, often claimed to be the biggest antiques market in the world, is outside the 18th arrondissement, but it's just a stone's throw beyond the Montmartre boundary. This huge flea-market-cum-antique-market is officially open on Saturdays, Sundays and Mondays. What does it sell? 'Everything' is the answer: everything from traffic lights to t-shirts. This massive site is actually a collection of over a dozen adjacent markets – just under 2000 shops/stalls in all.

Other places to go and see

Montmartre vineyard

Paris's only vineyard is on the north side of the Butte, looked after with love by a stern association of local wine aficionados. This tiny enterprise produces over 1000 bottles each harvest. Early each October the new vintage is celebrated loudly in a riotous vendage (harvest) festival.

Musée de Montmartre

A pleasant if low-key tribute to Montmartre's artistic heyday; with various period pieces, photos and memorabilia. The museum is mostly worth visiting for its excellent location and views over Northern Paris.

Montmartre Cemetery

This green, overgrown and slightly down-at-heel cemetery, sited low down in the hollow of an old quarry, is the last resting place of Degas, Dumas, Berlioz, Offenbach and others, but it particularly noted for the graves of Nijinsky and other balletic greats. Old ballet shoes are often left as tributes.

South Pigalle

South Pigalle, now nicknamed SoPi, is one of the most stylish new shopping areas, and epitomises the BoBo (bourgeois bohemian) Parisian lifestyle. Lots of ice-cool restaurants, bars and shops in what used to be a rather sleazy part of town. Streets to check out include rue des Martyrs, a bustling paradise for food-lovers, and rue Clauzel, SoPi's fashion street.

Moulin Rouge

The Moulin Rouge is synonymous with 'gay Paris' in the late 19th century: the can-can, Toulouse-Lautrec, ladies of loose morals, and so on. Today, a visit to the Moulin Rouge is still very popular with adult visitors to Paris, though of course it has now cleaned up its act, and offers a top-end cabaret, with dozens of performers in scanty costumes generously adorned with feathers, rhinestones, and sequins. If this is to your taste, then the famous Red Windmill is the place for you.

montmartre's cafe culture is iconic of paris

Chapter 20
Paris East Side: 19th & 20th Arrondissements

17th		18th		19th	
		9th	10th	11th	20th
	8th	2nd	3rd		
16th		1st	4th	12th	
	7th	6th	5th	13th	
	15th	14th			

Away from the centre, you can find a Paris of contrasts and surprises: wander the serene city parks, then stride the busy zig-zag streets; this is a different Paris – a secret city buzzing with activity and full of life.

In the 1940s, this was Edith Piaf's neighbourhood, a place for the working class and immigrants. Today, though, Belleville is an up-and-coming district with chic bohemian residents and its own distinctive cosmopolitan style. These city areas have also been settled by sizeable ethnic populations, especially North Africans, Malians, Turks and Chinese, making it one of the most diverse areas of the city and an excellent place for sampling exotic cuisine.

There are several large city parks on the east side; each is very different, and each merits a look around.

Headlines and highlights

Parc des Buttes-Chaumont

Perfect for Parisian picnics, packed with lanes, lawns, waterfalls and grottos. This large park was designed by Baron Haussman in the 19th century. Don't miss the bridges – including the charmingly named 'pont des Suicides' – and the mock-Greek temple sited on a rocky cliff with panoramic views over the city.

Children may be delighted to learn that before it was a park, this area was a rubbish tip; and before that it was a site for public hangings...

The Science Museum

Sited in the Parc de la Villette, the Cité des Sciences et de l'Industrie brands itself as a 'different kind of museum'. The biggest science museum in Europe, it contains a planetarium, an IMAX theatre, and an impressive collection of interactive, hands-on, scientifically engaging exhibits - a modern and diverting suburban contrast to the city-centre art-history-binge. Highlights include the spherical steel building itself, and the fifty metre Argonaute, a 1950s naval submarine.

Père Lachaise Cemetery

If you're French, famous, and dead – this is the place for you. With its grid layout, cobbled lanes and cast-iron signposts, the graveyard has the feel of a small nineteenth-century town, but in practice it is more like an exclusive nightclub: a long waiting list of people who want to get in, and strict criteria for who is allowed on the 'guest list' for admission. Luckily these rules don't apply if you're still alive, and the cemetery is one of Paris's most-visited locations.

Beautifully landscaped, with old trees overhanging mossy catacombs, the graveyard is a pleasure to visit, even without the joy of star-spotting: Molière, Jim Morrison, Frédéric Chopin, Oscar Wilde; Marcel Proust, Edith Piaf, Isadora Duncan, Gertrude Stein, Maria Callas, Modigliani...

Fans should note that Mr Morrison's tomb is regularly guarded, due to excessive graffiti, while Oscar Wilde's memorial – an Art Deco sculpture – has had to be repaired and encased in glass: so many of his admirers kissed the stone while wearing red lipstick that permanent damage was being caused to the tomb.

The cemetery also holds the Communards' Wall (Mur des Fédérés). This is the site where 147 Communards, the last defenders of the workers' district of Belleville, were shot on 28 May 1871 – the last day of the Week of Blood (Semaine Sanglante) in which the Paris Commune was crushed

Other places to go and see

Parc de Belleville

The highest park in Paris; this offers grand views over the city, and renowned floral displays - not to mention open-air ping-pong tables. There is also a small museum – the Maison de l'Air – extolling the virtues of fresh air.

Cité de la Musique

In the heart of the Parc de la Villette, the Museum of Music is dedicated to the history of western music, and contains over a thousand musical instruments including thos4e owned by famous 19th century composer Frederic Chopin and renowned 20th century virtuoso Frank Zappa.

Rue de Belleville

One of the most cosmopolitan places to eat and meet in Paris: good Chinese restaurants, Kosher food shops (mostly run by Tunisian Sephardic Jews) and Algerian pastry stalls. A vibrant and lively working-class shopping street; these working-class roots run deep: in 1871 this was the site of the Paris Commune's last barricade. Edith Piaf's birthplace is also on this street at No 72.

Parc de la Villette

Both of the museums mentioned above – the science museum and the museum of music – are sited in the Parc de la Villette, which merits a mention on its own account. In addition to its museums, the park houses concert halls, live performance stages, and theatres, as well as playgrounds for children, and no less than thirty-five architectural follies. The park itself comprises a collection of ten themed gardens. You may puzzle at what these themes are, and the official answer is that 'each garden is created with a different representation of architectural deconstruction-ism and tries to create space through different playfully sculptural means.' The children's playgrounds, though, are straightforward and easy to understand.

Conclusion
Aren't You Excited? Your Journey Is About to Begin!

It's time for your journey to begin. Maybe you're waiting for the Eurostar at London's St Pancras station, burning with curiosity about the incredible city waiting for you on the other side of the channel. Maybe you've just booked your flight, or your hotel – and are staring at the confirmation email buzzing with excitement. You might have just sat down at your first Parisian cafe, staring out at a view saturated with a surreal pick of the planet's greatest monuments and nursing the best glass of wine you've ever tasted.

Welcome to Paris – a city which holds a charismatic blend of Old World aloofness and the progressive ouevre of a modern metropolis. Trends are set here, revolutions are started, centuries-old traditions are honoured and local recipes are handed down through generations. Paris will seduce you, and hold you in its timeless grip.

Visiting Paris will cast a magic spell on you, whether its your first or your fifteenth visit. Go once and you will be mesmerised by monuments which have jumped straight off the pages of books and the silver screen into your vision; by a storied culture and history which you won't fully appreciate until you are in its midst. Go again, and again, and discover hidden corners, evolving suburbs and shifting counter-culture; indulgent food and an inspiring art scene which will continue to unfold, the harder you try to discover it.

See you in Paris – and then see you again.

LEARN FRENCH 300% FASTER

>> Get The Full French Online Course With Audio Lessons <<

If you truly want to learn French 300% FASTER, then hear this out.

I've partnered with the most revolutionary language teachers to bring you the very best French online course I've ever seen. It's a mind-blowing program specifically created for language hackers such as ourselves. It will allow you learn French 3x faster, straight from the comfort of your own home, office, or wherever you may be. It's like having an unfair advantage!

The Online Course consists of:

+ 211 Built-In Lessons
+ 99 Interactive Audio Lessons
+ 24/7 Support to Keep You Going

The program is extremely engaging, fun, and easy-going. You won't even notice you are learning a complex foreign language from scratch. And before you realize it, by the time you go through all the lessons you will officially become a truly solid French speaker.

Old classrooms are a thing of the past. It's time for a language revolution.

If you'd like to go the extra mile, then follow the link below, and let the revolution begin

>> http://www.bitly.com/French-Course <<

CHECK OUT THE COURSE »

PS: Can I Ask You a Quick Favor?

If you liked the book, please leave a nice review on Amazon! I'd absolutely love to hear your feedback. Every time I read your reviews... you make me smile. I'd be immensely thankful if you go to Amazon now, and write down a quick line sharing with me your experience. I personally read ALL the reviews there, and I'm thrilled to hear your feedback and honest motivation. It's what keeps me going, and helps me improve everyday =)

Please go Amazon now and drop a quick review sharing your experience!

***

THANKS!

***

ONCE YOU'RE BACK,
FLIP THE PAGE!
BONUS CHAPTER AHEAD
=)

Preview Of "England *For Tourists - The Traveler's Travel Guide to Make the Most Out of Your Trip to England - Where to Go, Eat, Sleep & Party*"

Introduction
Are You Ready for an Amazing Journey?

Welcome to England, a tiny island packed full of the extraordinary and the charming. Welcome to a country where no two experiences are the same. Gaze up at famous London landmarks then wander through deserted forest and rolling farmland. Spend an afternoon in an alternative working class suburb before enjoying an evening engrossed in Shakespeare. Discover the home of the Beatles and then discover the insides of a traditional English pub. England offers something for everyone, yet at its heart, is a very authentic and quintessential experience. Cream tea and scones, pork pies, flat caps, girls wearing short skirts in winter; the country stoically maintains its bizarre traditions and peculiar styles. No matter how much the scenery and accents change, an indelible imprint of Englishness follows you at every turn.

But what is England? Even the locals aren't so sure. Perhaps the country of quaint village greens and eating fish and chips along a pebbled beach. Maybe the chaotic buzz of the capital, or the trendy neighborhoods you'll find on its outskirts. Is it the Queen and the wonderful stately homes that dot the countryside? Manchester United, fried breakfasts, gothic cathedrals, Big Ben, cups of tea, more cups of tea, cobblestone streets of delight and intrigue; exploring England provides a continual immersion in both the famous and the unusual, the idiosyncratic and the popular. But the country's greatest appeal is its size. England is tiny and far smaller than most visitor's realize. Cramming a lot into a few days is relatively easy. First timers are quickly enchanted, while regular visitors always have something new to discover.

This guidebook has a very English approach at its heart. It's straightforward and to the point, providing the information you need to effectively plan and travel to the country. After all, when there is so much to discover and decipher, you need a guide that doesn't waffle or meander. Yet at the same time it likes to indulge in the eccentric, evoking authentic England and ensuring you seek out everything from your English experience. Think of it as a local holding your hand, guiding and revealing, but never demanding or forcing. Think of it as a fish and chip packet getting warm on your lap, sitting by a log fire in a country pub, or watching a musical in West End London. This guide is here to assist and support, but ensure England is always *your* experience.

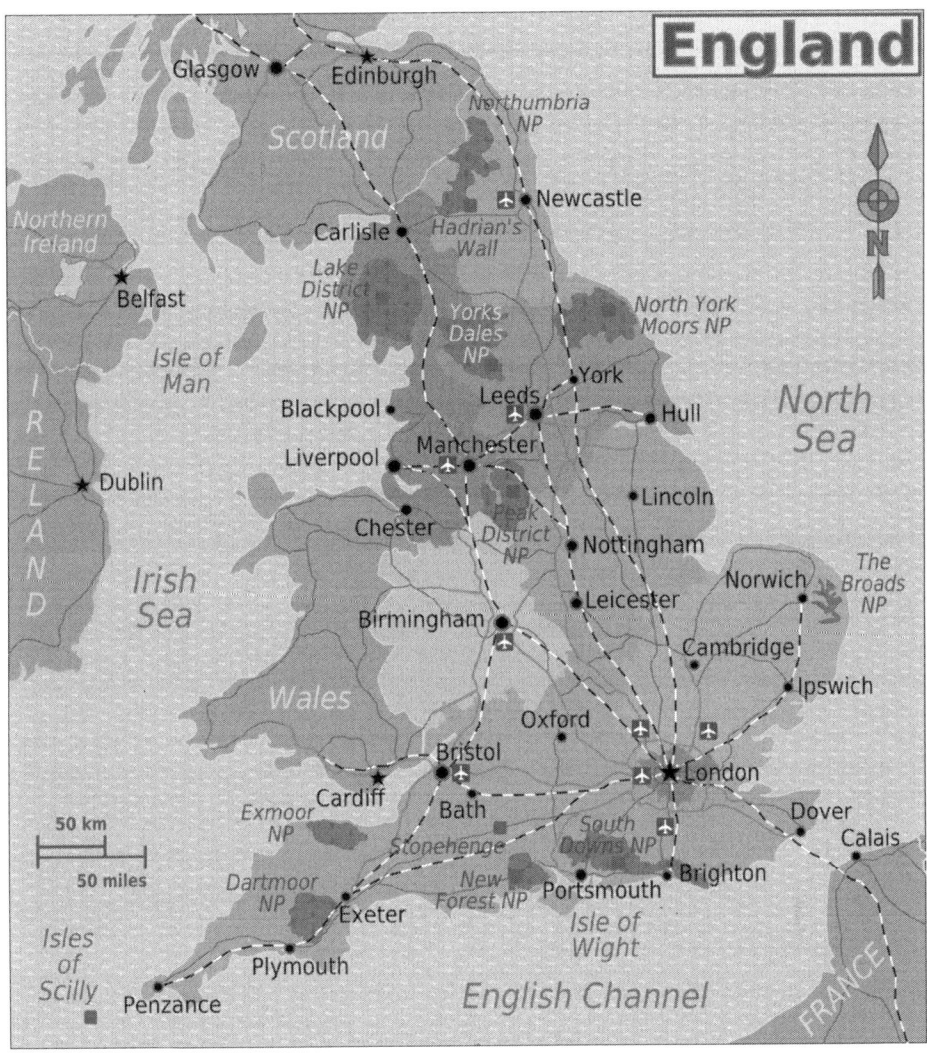

This is a country that everyone has to visit at least once in a lifetime, but which way do you turn? For some it's following a single paradigm, recreating the famous scenes from movies or shows like Downtown Abbey. Others plan more geographically, connecting the country's excellent transport network and dipping into a dozen compellingly different destinations. There's the visitor who wants a rural scene; dry stone walls, countless sheep, and endless hiking trails. Then let's not forget the mad glory of central London. This guide covers it all, north to south, east to west, and every odd little part in between. Oh, and it's written by a local...you were looking for the real English experience right?

Let's get started!

Chapter 1
Welcome to the Mighty England!

Most visitors land in London, the huge capital city that has enough to keep people entertained for months. Central London is where you'll find the infamous monuments and sights; Big Ben, Buckingham Palace, red double decker buses passing by St Paul's Cathedral... It's tourist central but it's quite wonderful. London actually constitutes of a multitude of distinct neighborhoods. Head to East London for vibrant working class suburbs that have become very cool. Go west for upmarket shopping and luxuriant districts, north for glimpses of classic old London, and south for a mix of it all.

Within an easy day trip of London you'll discover Southeast England, a historic place of medieval towns, world heritage sites, and alternative cities. Oxford, Canterbury, Brighton; choose to base yourself in London or leave the capital and easily tour these unique attractions.

Head Southwest and the rolling green farmlands of England begin to dominate the scene. It's quite a journey, the rural land packed with quaint stone villages, Neolithic rocks, and the country's best beaches. It's serene and enigmatic, each stop dancing with color and intimacy.

The Midlands is England's forgotten land, a cultural melting pot that most people merely skip through on route to The North. What it lacks in famous attractions it makes up for in delightful national parks, literary history, and intriguing cities.

If Scotland had voted for independence from the UK then The North would have tried to do the same. It's where you'll find England at its quintessentially bizarre best; strange accents, funny traditions, post-industrial cities, and historic market towns. This is the home of English popular music, God's own country (Yorkshire), famous football teams, and huge swathes of picturesque national park. Yes, it rains a lot here, but it's worth it.

England Highlights

Before you go head first into this guide let's indulge in the variety that England can provide. Here are selections of both the iconic and indelibly unique experiences you can discover.

Iconic Experiences

- Keep gasping in delight as you explore Central London and come face to face with all the classic scenes. Double decker buses, the Houses of Parliament, Tower Bridge, bright red phone boxes, Piccadilly Circus, then savor it all from the top of the London Eye. You won't meet many locals, but you'll fill the camera roll with dozens of famous sights. *(see Chapter 4: London)*

- Wander the cute medieval streets of Oxford, reveling in the illustrious history of this stunning university town. Once you're done admiring the buildings and cathedral, step inside atmospheric taverns and explore side-streets that dance with charm. *(see Chapter 5: Around London and Southeast England)*

- Go back in time and stand before the great Neolithic rocks of Stonehenge, an ancient riddle that historians are still struggling to solve. Nowhere can better exemplify the time travel conundrum of England, particularly if you've come straight from the city lights of London. *(see Chapter 6: Southwest England)*

- Get lost in the rolling hills of the Peak District National Park. Hike along deserted country trails and then reappear besides a cute traditional pub. For a remote escape into rural England it's hard to find a more fitting place. *(see Chapter 7: The Midlands)*

- Go on a musical tinged journey through Liverpool, feasting your eyes on the Victorian monuments before a *Magical Mystery Tour* reveals the hometown of the Beatles. Even at 2pm on a Wednesday you can be singing along in the atmospheric cavern where the fab four first performed. *(see Chapter 8: The North)*

Unique Experiences

- Get on the underground and alight in East London, full of once dingy neighborhoods that now burst with color, creativity, and England's modern multiculturalism. Wander down the Bangladeshi influenced Brick Lane, explore graffiti covered pop-up shops and markets, and discover where real Londoners go to hang out. *(see Chapter 4: London)*

- Dip your feet into the sand of Brighton beach and then experience the city's desire to promote alternative culture. It's hard to find a more entertaining night out than Brighton, then again, it's difficult to go ten minutes without spotting something funky or weird along the open promenade. *(see Chapter 5: Around London and Southeast England)*

- Indulge in the ancient splendor of Bath, a city that's a living UNESCO World Heritage site and a museum space of abbeys, arched bridges, glorious townhouses, and Roman baths. For artistic beauty, few cities in the world can match Bath's Georgian painting (see Chapter 6: Southwest England)

- Alight in Nottingham and feast your eyes on the juxtaposition of modern England. You'll find old cathedrals, glistening shopping centers, cobbled streets, and bustling city bars. It's all well off the tourist trail, just remember to say "eyup duck," the local slang for "hello." (see Chapter 7: The Midlands)

- Forgive the grey skies as you amble through the winding roads of the Lake District, exploring green valleys punctuated by too many sheep and some serene lakes. The landscape here is as English as a cup of tea, and it won't be long before you're chatting with the locals about the weather (see Chapter 8: The North)

The bucolic landscapes of the Lake District

This guide is split into three distinct sections. Each is designed to offer the most essential information to both plan and maximize your experience. England is a relatively easy country to travel in. The transport infrastructure is excellent, as is the choice of hotels and availability of tourist information offices. This guide offers the shortcuts and need to know, without polluting essential information with the unnecessary. It is designed with every type of visitor in mind, and covers common interests and destinations. At the same time, it places a heavy emphasis on helping visitors discover authentic England and sidestep overpriced overhyped attractions.

What you won't find in this guide is very detailed information on individual hotels, entry ticket prices, or establishment phone numbers. Instead, the general information is explained and you're directed to the best sources of information. For example, there are thirty or so small bed and breakfast hotels in the city of York. Almost every visitor will stay in one of these "B & B's" and they all essentially offer the same experience.

Chapter 2 provides all the information you require to plan your trip to England. It discusses classic travel routes and potential itineraries, when to go, how much it's going to cost, and basic travel requirements. Whole section are dedicated to getting around and cutting down costs. Public transport can cost 90% less if you book it in advance, so you need to know about it before you arrive in the country. You'll also find information on the best ways to travel between regions. This chapter also details the accommodation types and standard options for getting a good night's sleep.

Chapter 3 is about maximizing your experience and immersing yourself in English culture. Things like what to eat, what to drink, remembering your manners, and staying safe. Strange mannerisms and customs are what make England so great, so it's worth having an overview before you land on the fair isle.

Chapters 4 - 8 provide detailed information about each destination. These chapters are divided into five geographical regions. Every destination is presented in the same way. You'll be introduced to the place and the experiences on offer. This quick succinct style should provide enough information for you to make an informed decision about whether it's a place to consider for your itinerary. Then the guide provides practical information to make your visit a reality, including how to get there, travel essentials, and how to orientate yourself on arrival.

[Click Here to Check out the Rest of "*England For Tourists*" on Amazon](#)

Check Out My Other Books

Are you ready to exceed your limits? Then pick a book from the one below and start learning yet another new language. I can't imagine anything more fun, fulfilling, and exciting!

If you'd like to see the entire list of language guides (there are a ton more!), go to:

>>http://www.amazon.com/Dagny-Taggart/e/B00K54K6CS/<<

About the Author

Dagny Taggart is a language enthusiast and polyglot who travels the world, inevitably picking up more and more languages along the way.

Taggart's true passion became learning languages after she realized the incredible connections with people that it fostered. Now she just can't get enough of it. Although it's taken time, she has acquired vast knowledge on the best and fastest ways to learn languages. But the truth is, she is driven simply by her motive to build exceptional links and bonds with others.

She is inspired everyday by the individuals she meets across the globe. For her, there's simply not anything as rewarding as practicing languages with others because she gets to make friends with people from all that come from a variety of cultures. This, in turn, has broadened her mind and thinking more than she would have ever imagined it could.

Of course, as a result of her constant travels, Taggart has become an expert on planning trips and making the most of time spent out of what she calls her "base" town. She jokes that she's practically at the nomad status now, but she's more content to live that way.

She knows how to live on a manageable budget weather she's in Paris or Phnom Penh. She knows how to seek out the adventures and thrills, no doubt, lying in wait at any city she visits. She knows that reflection on each every experience is significant if she wants to grow as a traveler and student of the world's cultures.

Because of this, Taggart chooses to share her understanding of languages and travel so that others, too, can experience the same life-altering benefits she has.

10712557R00065

Printed in Great Britain
by Amazon.co.uk, Ltd.,
Marston Gate.